Broken to Beautiful

by

KR Turner, LPC

2019

What people are saying about Broken to Beautiful

This book is both heart wrenching and compelling. As I finished reading it, I realized what a powerful tool it will be for others who have been victimized and abused. The author takes the reader on a journey of agony and despair, ending the journey with hope and triumph. This is a book I will recommend to any person who is battling the demons of abuse. I am going to order enough copies for the therapist, nursing staff, support staff, and psychiatrist at the Mental Health Outpatient Clinic where I work. This book is a must read.
Theresa Miller

Kimberly tells her story in a way that grips your heart. The way she explains her life circumstances is relatable and it helps you see things differently. She offers great insight and perspective based on her personal experiences and her studies as a professional therapist. This story and perspective is unlike anything else I've ever read and I highly recommend to anyone with children or who work with children.
Elizabeth Grimm
Functional Medicine Certified Health Coach

Kimberly has a such a beautifully authentic way of owning her story. Don't be surprised if you find yourself weeping with her and simultaneously celebrating her triumph. She has courageously lead us through the intricacies of surviving and overcoming the shattering effects of abuse. Thank you for holding out a lifeline of hope to those who have yet to overcome.
Tammy Claughton

"This unforgettable book is a must-read for anyone whose lives have been impacted by sexual abuse. May you find freedom and healing along the way."
Shelli Schilt, Board Certified Biblical Counselor, Lifepoint Church

In her book, Ms. Turner shares her painfully honest and heart wrenching story of sexual, physical, mental and emotional abuse. As a retired Department of Child Safety Case Manager, I worked with many abused children and saw first hand the devasting effects of abuse. Ms. Turner's story is one of hope, victory and redemption. It is a story of encounters with people who spoke words of truth, hope and encouragement into her brokenness. It is a story of God's redeeming love. While this book was difficult to read, it is a must read for all who work with abused children and troubled teens. Our words and actions make a difference.
Vickie P

"Kimberly Turner is a person with a story. An intense story. In these pages you will read of intense pain, graphic struggles, and what happens. What I love about Kimberly is that she is a person of hope. These pages will also include the redemptive message that what happens to you is not what defines you. What happens in you can give life through you. Read this book and get hope!"
Dr. John Jackson is the President of William Jessup University, a popular speaker, and an author of 6 books on leadership, culture, and transformation.

Broken to Beautiful
is available at special quantity discounts for bulk purchase for sales promotions,
premiums, fund-raising, and educational needs.
For details write Endurance Press, 577 N Cardigan Ave, Star, ID 83669.

Visit Endurance Press' website at www.endurancepress.com

Broken to Beautiful

PUBLISHED BY ENDURANCE PRESS
577 N Cardigan Ave
Star, ID 83669 U.S.A.

All rights reserved. Except for brief excerpts for review purposes,
no part of this book may be
reproduced or used in any form without
prior written permission from the publisher.

ISBN 978-1-733550314

®2019 Kimberly Turner

Cover by Teal Rose Design Studios

Interior by Endurance Press

Printed in the United States of America

First Edition 2019

Introduction

These are my memories. Everything you are about to read happened in my life.

This story tells it like it was. I did not change, exaggerate, or sugarcoat the details. Everything is as I remember; however, due to the traumatic nature of the events, there are gaps in my memory, as well as memories that are fragmented rather than complete. Because this is a factual account of my life, the language and details are raw and emotional. The book is written in the format of a diary. Background information is interspersed with diary entries to add clarity. Some of the events have been condensed to fit into one year of my life. The names of people have been changed.

My desire is that readers use my story of survival as a means to help themselves or others who are in a similar situation. Child abuse is a horrific way for any child to grow up, but it can be overcome. Because there were people in my life who cared, I was able to survive and eventually thrive. If I can overcome my childhood, so can others.

Prologue

Our new house just got finished, and we finally moved in. I have been playing in the tree house with my brother, sister, and some neighbor boys. Daddy walks down the path of the forest and begins to scream in anger at the boys. "Leave now, and I never want to see you around my daughter again!" Then he looks at my brother and sister. "Go home now! I'll deal with you when I get home." He is mad. "They should not have taken you into the tree house. You're too little to be up there." He climbs into the tree house. His face is red, and I am scared of his anger. He starts to yell, "Boys are bad! You are NEVER to be alone with boys. I need to show you what boys want from you!"

He starts to undo his belt, and I know he is going to whip me, but he does not take it out of the belt loops. He pulls down his pants and points at his privates, yelling about how bad boys are and he needs to show me. He throws me on my back and pulls my pink shorts around my ankles. He is ripping me apart; the pain is so bad. I am crying and trying to get away. He holds me down with his arms and legs. I feel the wood ripping apart my bottom and back as he rips apart my insides. The pounding goes on and on.

My shoe slips off my foot, and I hear it land on the earth below. He finally stands up, wipes something from between my legs with his handkerchief, and pulls my shorts up. He says, "Go get your shoe and put it back on." He waits at the bottom of the tree as I climb down. I hear his foot tapping and know I need to hurry. He carries me back to the house. I am crying from the pain. He tells me, "Stop crying. It doesn't hurt. It's a good thing I came to rescue you from the tree house. You were too scared to get down and I saved you."

I am confused. I wasn't afraid of the tree house. I was having fun.

We get home and he tells Mommy, "She was stuck in the tree house. I had to rescue her. It took a long time to get her down because she was so scared. I had to climb up to carry her. When we were coming down, her back got scraped. She needs a bath."

Mommy gets up to run my bath, but daddy tells her to rest. He will take care of me. I wish Mommy would give me my bath. Daddy puts me in the water—it's too hot and it hurts, but I don't cry. He will hit me if I cry. He always makes the water too hot, and he always scrubs too hard.

Daddy starts to wash me. Maybe it won't hurt this time. He tells me, "I love you so much. It's important for you to stay clean all the time. I'll make sure you are always clean and pretty." When he is done with my hair, he tells me to stand up. Then he soaps up his hands extra good. My breath stops.

He starts with my face and his hands move lower. He passes my bottom and washes my legs and feet. He rinses his hands—I breathe again. I turn to let the water out.

"Wait, Princess, I'm not done. You must be clean everywhere." He re-soaps his hands, turns me around, and washes my bottom, and then he turns me back around to face him. His hands wash my front, getting inside and out.

His fingers snake ever higher. The soap stings and his fingers hurt me inside where I am already torn in two. I start to cry. It comes from nowhere—SMACK!

"Stop crying! It doesn't hurt. We have to make sure you are clean!"

I try not to cry, and he tells me I am a good girl.

He rinses me, then dries me off, everywhere. The towel hurts between my legs. I still feel like I am being ripped apart. He puts my pajamas on, takes me to Mommy so I can say goodnight, and then tucks me in bed.

"Good night, Princess. Daddy loves you so much."

I hear him going down the hall. I hear him yelling at David. I hear the sound of the belt hitting flesh, first in David's room, then in Daphne's. I know they will never take me to the tree house again. I cry myself to sleep because I hurt inside where daddy showed me what boys do and where he washed me.

I am four years old.

***

Daddy has his own house in the city now, and Mommy drives me there for the weekend. It is a really far drive. I am tired by the time we get there. I didn't sleep well. I threw up when I was sleeping again.

Mommy was mad. She yelled, "Why do you keep throwing up. Stop crying! I'm not doing anything to you! Put your sheets in the washer and go take a shower! Because you made a mess, you get to stay up and finish your wash. Make your bed when it's done, and don't go back to bed until you finish!"

I try not to throw up, but I can't help it, and I don't understand why she's mad at me.

We get to daddy's house. Mommy doesn't even wait until we get to his apartment. She just drives away.

I go and put my clothes in his room. Daddy takes us to the mini-golf place, and we play two courses. It's fun, but I'm not thinking about having fun. I want to go back to my Mommy's house.

We go to Bob's Big Boy for lunch. I get a shrimp basket, my favorite. Daddy flirts with the waitress. He comes here a lot. They all know him. He gets a Bob's Big Boy and a cup of coffee. His breath always smells like coffee, cigarettes, and the whiskey he drinks at home.

After lunch, we go home and go to the pool. We swim all afternoon. Daddy teaches me how to dive. He is so proud of how quickly I learn. "Great job, Princess!" He turns to the lady sitting next to him on the lounge chairs. "Look how smart and pretty she is. She just learned to dive today."

The lady looks at me and smiles. I smile back and wave. Daddy is proud of me. I've been a good girl.

After we swim, we go back to the apartment. Daddy makes dinner: salad with pickles, tomatoes, and mayonnaise, baked chicken, and french fries. It tastes pretty good. I am happy. I have been a good girl today. Daddy tells me to go put on my nightgown.

After dinner, we sit in the living room and watch TV. David has some friends from the pool over. Daddy calls me over to his lap. I crawl on and curl up. We sit for a while, and then daddy stretches me out on top of him, my tummy on his. He rubs my back, and I start to fall asleep.

Then daddy's hand starts to rub my bottom. I squirm away. He gets mad and tells me to be still. I ask him to stop rubbing. He gets really mad and sends me to bed.

I wait in his bed. He comes in, takes off his belt, and hits me everywhere. I don't know what I did wrong. I was such a good girl today. The hitting doesn't stop. He yells at me for disobeying and being such a bad girl. He holds the belt so that the buckle hits me.

I have learned not to move. It just makes it worse. I cry silently as the blows rain down on my tiny body. After every inch of my back and legs has been struck, he stops, puts his belt back on, and walks out of the room.

I pray to a God that I heard about that one time we went to church. "God, why is my daddy always mad at me? Help me to be good."

I try to stay awake. Sleeping is dangerous. I lie on my stomach, pressing myself as tightly as I can to the bed. I wrap myself up in the covers. Stay awake, stay awake, I tell myself. It is useless. I am tired and I sleep. I wake from a nightmare; I am so scared.

I feel my hand around something hard and wet. I am on my back. Daddy is over me. It's not a nightmare. It is my reality. The nightmare doesn't end when I wake.

I am five years old. Is there a God to answer my prayers?

Daddy's Girl

*He used to call me princess
and pull me on his lap,
put his hand in my panties
and tell me how much he loved me.*

*He used to come in when I was taking a bath.
He would wash carefully
every nook and cranny
and tell me how much he loved me.*

*He used to come into my bed
and place my tiny hand around his manhood,
stifle my cries with his hand,
and tell me how much he loved me.*

*He used to take me aside for his pleasure.
He taught me how to French kiss
and threatened harm if I told,
and tell me how much he loved me.*

*He used to call me princess.
He used me for his sin
and told me it was because he loved me.*
     I HATE HIM

Family and Homes

I am the baby of the family. There is Dad, Mom, David, Daphne, and me. Mom and Dad got a divorce when I was in Kindergarten, I think. I can't really remember. There are a lot of things I don't remember. But I do remember the fights, especially the last one.

Mom and dad were yelling. Mom sent us kids to our rooms and told us to lock our doors and not let anyone in. I never heard them yell that way before. I was really scared. I heard hitting and things crashing and I was scared that he was hitting her the way he hit me. I wanted to go out and protect her, but she told me to stay in my room. I didn't know what to do.

Finally, the noise stopped. Mom told us it was okay, he'd left, but I knew it wasn't okay. She went to her room and told us to stay in ours. He never came back to the house, and we had to visit him in the city. David went to live with him. I don't know why he had to go. Why couldn't all of us kids stay together?

I grew up in the Santa Cruz Mountains. We had a big house with lots of room to explore. My favorite part of the house was the deck. I remember the house being built and playing in the frame of the house. You could see the ocean and the light reflecting off of the Big Dipper Rollercoaster on the boardwalk all the way in Santa Cruz. We had a lot of property and no close neighbors. I could explore the woods and escape from home whenever I needed to.

My favorite place away from the house was the oak tree. I would climb up, sit in the crook of two branches, and just be by myself. There was also a huge boulder I would sit on. I had to crawl through bushes to get there, and it was hard for anyone but me to get on the boulder because the bushes were tight. The bushes were also full of daddy longlegs, but they didn't bother me. I was little so I could worm my way through the bushes. When I got on the boulder, I just brushed the spiders off. It felt safe.

Before the house in the mountains, we lived in another house. I hated that house. One time I had a nightmare that was so real. I was screaming and my mom came in my room. Someone had come into my room and had tried to get me. There was a trail of blood from my crib to the window, and my window was open. Actually, I am not sure if it was a nightmare or real. It felt real and made me afraid of that house. I must have been pretty little since I was still in a crib. I will never forget that—I get scared inside just thinking about it. Sometimes I wonder if the person who was trying to get me was my dad and I just blocked it all out.

My school, LP Elementary School, was a country school that included grades from Kindergarten through eighth-grade. The town built a junior high school across the street when I was in second grade. The high school was in Los Gatos.

I liked Kindergarten. I built block houses and hid in them. I got to paint, and sing, and play outside. I already knew all of my letters and could read. It was fun. But after Kindergarten, things changed. I mostly hated my teachers in elementary school. They wouldn't let me read, even though my mom told them to let me read whatever I wanted. The books were baby books, and I wasn't a baby. Didn't they know that?

I got into a lot of fights in school. I would beat up anyone who was mean to me or someone else. I beat up this sixth-grade boy because he teased me. I was only in second grade, but I was so tough. When I got in trouble, the principal was always nice. I would rather sit with him than be in class, where I couldn't concentrate anyway. He used to just talk to me and try to figure out what was wrong. My mom never figured out why I got in so many fights at school. I never knew why either until I got older and figured out I was mad at my father. Too bad everyone was so clueless!

At the end of my fourth-grade year, my mom sold our house in the mountains and bought a house in San Jose. School wasn't over, so I stayed with a family my mom knew until summer vacation. They were awesome. Their names were Phillip and Melissa. They had a little girl, Rebekah.

Every night, they read bedtime stories to Rebekah and let me listen. I don't think I had ever had a story read to me by my parents. I always remember reading to myself. I don't know when I learned to read. I can't remember not reading.

They had a big garden, and Melissa stayed home while Phillip worked. It was like a real family. Melissa let me help in the kitchen and with chores. At home, I did most chores myself. No one ever helped. I just got yelled at and hit if I didn't do it exactly right.

Phillip and Melissa were painting their bathroom and let me help paint everywhere I could reach. It was so cool that they trusted me not to make a mistake. I also got to help them in the garden. They had gophers but didn't want to kill them, so we tried all sorts of things to get rid of them.

One night, I had a nightmare and couldn't sleep. I got up to go to the bathroom, and Phillip was up. He was just going outside to see if he could catch the gopher. He let me go out with him. I felt safe. That was really cool. I missed them when school was over. Actually, I guess I missed the whole family thing.

I hated San Jose from the minute I moved there. It was dirty and loud. There were no trees to climb or places to hide. I missed the mountains more than anyone could ever imagine. Daphne loved the city and made friends right away. She didn't miss the mountains at all. I spent all summer playing with a four-year-old next door because I didn't know anyone. His parents were just happy he had someone to amuse him. They used to let me babysit for a couple of hours while they went grocery shopping and ran errands.

I hated the house in San Jose, too. The first month we were there, someone threw a rock through my window when I was alone in the house. I was so scared. Mom just told me to grow up. She got it fixed. I think it was Daphne's stupid friends.

The house was right on the corner of a busy street. The noise from the cars and trucks never stopped, even in the middle of the night. Speaking of nights, my mom worked the night shift, so I was alone all night, every night. Daphne went to parties every night. I hated being alone worse than I hated being with my family.

I had a waterbed platform bed, and there was a crawl

space in the front between the wall and the bed and another crawl space at the foot of the bed between the drawers on the side. When I got scared at night, I would crawl into one of those spaces and sleep in there so that if anyone came into the house, they wouldn't find me.

I also had a whole bunch of stuffed animals on my bed. I set them up every night to surround me. I would crawl in the middle of this fortress of animals and feel safe. I knew they couldn't really keep me safe, but it helped me feel less scared when I was alone at night.

The year we moved to San Jose was the year that Daphne started to be mean to me. She had no use for me, only for her friends. She and her friends got a real kick out of torturing me. One time, they threw me outside, and, as I put my hand on the sliding glass door to get back in, Daphne slammed the door on my thumb. It almost cut my thumb off. I was screaming, and she was yelling for me to shut up. Her friend Karley told her to open the door. When Karley saw my bloody thumb, she got scared. Her mom was a nurse, so she took me over to her house to get it bandaged up. Daphne never even said she was sorry. She just threatened to beat the crap out of me if I told mom.

I hated my school, AT Elementary School. I had to walk forever to get there. I missed the long bus ride and the quietness of the mountains. My teacher was okay though. I guess the thing about that school I remember the most is how stupid I was. We were learning fractions, and I just couldn't get it.

Thinking back, I guess it was because I couldn't concentrate during school. I was always worried about going home or to my dad's house. During math, we all had to take turns at the board and write out the answers to the math problems. I would stare at the board, feeling everyone's eyes on me. I would try to write something, erase it because I knew it was wrong, and then just write something, anything, so I could go back to my seat. I could never do it, and all the kids teased me. The teacher tried to help, but I just couldn't wrap my mind around the whole math thing.

The one part of the day I did like was English. I wrote a story about going to a bubblegum factory, and the teacher hung it on the board because it was so good. I guess I have always liked to write.

I made a friend at that school, but she turned out to be a real piece of work. We used to play family and pretend we were fashion models. In the family game, I was the teen and the closet was my room. Then we played model. She would take pretend pictures of me. One day when we were playing, she kissed me on the mouth. I punched her in the face, and the next day I told everyone at school that she was a lesbian. Thinking back, I shouldn't have told everyone. It sucks to have everyone tease you. That was mean of me.

I had another friend at AT Elementary School, Elise. I spent a lot of time at her house. It took forever to walk there, but it was nice being with her family. Her mom cooked the best Mexican food and Elise and I would wash the dishes after dinner. I could go to Elise's house whenever I wanted. My mom didn't care I was gone as long as I let her know where I was going. Sometimes I spent the night at her house, but I never wanted her to spend the night at my house. I just told her my sister was mean. Elise was nice to me, but I thought if she knew about the real me, the me that I didn't share with anyone, she would hate me. So

I played games, pretended I was happy, and pretended that the real me didn't exist.

I always got in fights at my new school. I hated everything about that school and the differences between a city school and a country school. At my old school, we would have class outside and learn about nature. The only time we got to go outside at the city school was for recess, and then only if the weather was nice.

It was almost the end of my fifth-grade year, and I was in the principal's office once again. My mom came in and told me if I got in one more fight, or if she got one more call from the school, she would put me in a foster home. I never got into another fight. Looking back, I wish I would have gotten in more fights. My life probably would have been a lot different.

It was in San Jose, right before I went into sixth grade, that I told my mom about what my dad had been doing to me all those years. After he and my brother moved to the city, I went to visit every weekend. I told my mom that he had made me sleep in his bed when I was there and I didn't like it. I told her, "He does sex things to me." I don't think she ever really believed me. The only thing that was different after I told her was that I didn't see my dad for a couple of months. When I did see him again, he came to my house and my mom would disappear into the back bedroom or go to the store. Sometimes he would take me out to lunch or the movies, but I didn't have to stay the night with him anymore. At least, that is what I thought would happen.

My mom sent me to summer school between fifth and sixth grade so I'd be out of the house. I took two classes: lab science and art. I liked that I had something to do and that I didn't have to be alone in the house.

There was this boy who always bullied me. I didn't really know why. One day, while we were doing an experiment in science class, he held my arm down on the hot plate we used to boil water. I screamed and swore at him. The teacher grabbed me by the arm. I thought I was in trouble, but she just brought me to the nurse. I told her I was sorry for swearing, but she told me it was okay because it must have hurt. I got second-degree burns on my arm, and the boy was kicked out of summer school. Mom acted like it was a big hassle to take me to the emergency room to get my arm fixed.

On the playground at school, there was a big pile of tires all connected with bolts. On the first day of sixth grade, I was sitting on the tires with some other kids, and the jerk boy who'd burned me came over to the tires. He told everyone that I'd had sex with him in the tires at summer school and that I was a total slut. They all believed him. What a jerk! I wanted to fight him so bad, but I wasn't going to fight anymore. So, the first day of sixth grade I had a reputation I didn't deserve.

It didn't really matter though because, less than a month later, we moved again.

JS Elementary School

We moved from San Jose to Santa Clara. The house wasn't so bad. It was in a quiet neighborhood. My school, JS Elementary, was a good school. Because I was in sixth grade, I had three teachers instead of just one. My favorite was Mrs. Molere. She was awesome. She put me on the safety patrol. That was fun. We had to get to school early, put up the flag, and help the little kids cross the street. We got out of the last class of the day a little earlier than everyone else so we could help the kids cross the street again, and then we had to take the flag down and put it away. I liked safety patrol. It was really fun. We sang a marching song and we had a certain ceremony for putting up and taking down the flag. More than liking safety patrol, I really liked that Mrs. Molere trusted me.

I started to make friends at this school. Tina and Sarah both had good families. Morgan's mom was divorced, and she had a boyfriend. Her boyfriend was steady though, not like my mom, with her endless line of men parading through her bedroom door. I also had friends in my neighborhood: Stefan, Tobey, Ian, and Troy. There were school friends and neighbor friends. Each group of friends required a certain way to act. With Tina and Sarah, I acted like my family was great. I'm not even sure I told them my parents were divorced. I could be more real with Morgan because her mom was divorced. With the boys in the neighborhood, I had to prove I was tough and not let them push me around.

    Santa Clara became my home. Even though I missed the mountains, things became easier with a somewhat steady home—for a while. The biggest improvement was that since I wasn't spending the night at my dad's, I didn't have to worry about what he would do to me.

LC Junior High

In the mountains, I knew everyone, but it was different in the city. When I went to LC Junior High, there were kids who had gone to other elementary schools. That was cool because they didn't know about my reputation—the reputation I had gotten from someone I thought was a friend, but that is another story.

The best part about LC Junior High was Mr. Dover. He was my counselor in seventh grade. I was supposed to have a new one in eighth grade, but he let me stay with him for both years. He asked once why I had got into so many fights at my old schools. I told him my dad hit me and I was mad all the time. He told me my dad was a jerk and that I didn't deserve what he did to me. The reason I liked Mr. Dover so much is that he was the first one to tell me the abuse wasn't my fault.

LC Junior High was a lot different than JS Elementary. There was the popular crowd, the beautiful people. Then there was the rest of us.

The best memory I have of LC Junior High is not really of school at all. Abraham, the youth pastor at my church, wanted to get the junior high kids more involved. There were a lot of activities for the high schoolers but not for the junior high kids. He started a club called Maranatha, which means "the Lord is coming." It was after school once a week.

My mom was working, so she didn't know if I got home late or not. I started to go to the meetings so I could learn more about this God thing. The meetings were at Timothy's house because it was close to the school. Timothy was one of the kids in the high school group and his parents tried to help the youth pastor however they could. So they let Abraham hold the meeting there, even though their son was already too old for the group. Although it was a small group, only 4 or 5 of us, it was fun. Every week we would have a Bible study, and then we would play silly games. Abraham bought this gigantic bag of popcorn, and Timothy's mom always made us snacks.

Maranatha was when I got close to Abraham. I started dropping small hints about my dad, but no real details. I told him things like my dad hit me and that he drank and that I was scared when I had to go there. I think I told him that I wasn't allowed to go to my dad's house for a while, but I thought I would have to go back someday because that happened before. The little bit I did say was enough for him also to tell me that what my dad did wasn't my fault. I asked a lot of questions about how the God he talked about could let bad stuff happen. He didn't really have an answer, but he didn't pretend to have an answer either. He was always honest with me. I loved Abraham like I had never loved anyone before. I always wished he was my dad.

When I cried, he would hug me, and I was never afraid. When I was down, he would encourage me. He once told me, "After you go through the fire, you will come out smelling like a rose." The first time he told me that, I told him that Rose was my middle name. He told me that God caused me to have that middle name to remind me of my beauty. No one had ever told me I had beauty inside. Abraham was the best ever. After a few years, he moved to a different city to become the pastor of a church there. I missed him much more than I let on to anyone.

Another good thing about Maranatha was Timothy. He would come home from high school and say hey to all of us. I think he thought I was just a little kid. I tried to prove him wrong by talking to him. I would always talk to him at church before we went to our separate youth groups. I couldn't wait to finish junior high and move up to the high school group because the junior high kids were so immature.

By the time I was in eighth grade, I was drinking every day and smoking pot almost every day. Since I'd moved to the city in fifth grade, drugs and drinking had just become a normal thing. I was always depressed. I really hated myself. I didn't know why I felt so bad about myself. I only knew that I hurt all the time and I wanted it to end. The only way I knew how to make the pain go away was to escape with alcohol and drugs.

The only good thing in my life was Maranatha and, by extension, Abraham, but I always felt like a fake. I was leading two different lives. The people closest to me didn't know how much I was partying. I had built a big wall and kept my secrets safely behind that wall. I didn't know how to let anyone inside. I was afraid that if I told Abraham how much I was partying, he wouldn't like me anymore. So, I became two different people: the party girl and the good girl.

My mom took me to Hawaii near the end of my eighth-grade year. All my friends were so jealous. I would have gladly let them go in my place. It was really nice there, but I couldn't shake the depression. To feel depressed in such a beautiful place really sucks.

One night I went to the ocean by myself. I walked down to the ocean thinking that it would be so easy to drown myself. I felt so peaceful and so happy that everything would be over. I knew my mom would be sad, well, I hoped so anyway, but I figured she would get over it quickly and move on. It wasn't like she really cared anyway. I can't even put a number on the times she told me I was a mistake and she wished I had never been born.

I was almost to the water when I stepped on a broken bottle and cut my foot open. I guess it brought me back to reality because I went back to where my mom was waiting at the restaurant and told her I had cut my foot on the beach. A waitress took me into the bathroom and bandaged my foot. That was the first time I seriously thought about killing myself. Although I didn't follow through with the attempt, I sincerely wanted to die and knew death was the only way to end the pain inside. I was thirteen years old.

My bad reputation continued to develop at LC Junior High. Even though I didn't fight, everyone knew I was tough and to leave me the heck alone. For some reason, everyone thought I was a slut. I really don't know what I did to deserve the reputation. I didn't sleep with anyone. I guess my supposed friend's little story followed me from JS Elementary School, but more on that later. I started not to care what people thought because there was nothing I could do about it anyway. At least, that's what Abraham told me. I tried to forget by drinking and smoking pot. It really didn't help much. I don't know why I kept doing the drugs. I guess any attempt at feeling better was worth the try.

PART 1

Summer Prior to Freshman Year

August 23
Dear Diary,

    I decided to start writing to see if it would help at all. Everyone tells me to get my feelings out - except Mom, "Pull yourself up by your bootstraps." What stupid bootstraps! That's an idiotic thing to say. Anyway, maybe if I write, I can figure out why I am such a mess. It is three weeks away from my 14th birthday. This is supposed to be such a big deal - but it just isn't. I wish it could be, but for me - life just isn't like everyone else's.

    Reid invited me over last night. He lives across the street and is Daphne's friend. I think he is 19. Anyway, whenever Daphne has parties, he is always making eyes at me. He was Celia's boyfriend, but they broke up. So - Mom was spending the night at her boyfriend's house again and I was alone as usual. I went over to Reid's. He has a room built above the garage, it is pretty cool. We drank a couple of beers and were messing around. He said he wanted to make love to me. Yeah, right. More like just sex. I agreed anyway, because who cares? I have never been a virgin, and I never will be. So what difference will it make, right? But I was a little scared, because - well, you know - it was the first time that I decided to have sex on my own. So I guess in reality, it is kinda important. Anyway - he was real gentle and stuff, so it didn't hurt. I guess I wanted it to hurt because maybe then I would be normal. He wanted to be all lovey-dovey after, but I just went home, at 3 a.m. Didn't matter, no one knows or cares where I go or what I do. I took a shower when I got home, just like daddy always taught me. I hurt inside. I didn't cry, because that's not something I do. I curled up with teddy and went to sleep.

   I feel so gross, disgusting and dirty this morning. Probably because my dad would be furious if he knew. Forget the creep! I can sleep with anyone I want! His days of using me are over. I am now a woman because I wanted to be, not because he decided he wanted sex. Maybe I feel bad because Grace will be disappointed. It's easy for her to say don't do drugs, don't drink, don't have sex. She has parents who care about her. I know she loves me and I don't want her to be upset with me - but it is just so hard to be good. It is so much easier to be bad. I am such a worthless creep.

Grace

After I told Mrs. Molere, my sixth-grade teacher, that my mom was sending me to stay with my dad, I had to have a babysitter. I'd been taking care of myself since I was like six, and then at twelve I had to have a sitter. It was so embarrassing.

Mom got the next-door neighbor, Mrs. Stoneboro, to watch me. It turned out that I liked having a babysitter. It was kind of like having a grandma, something I never had. She was awesome. We always baked cookies and had long talks.

The church around the corner was having a day camp. I said I would go because Mrs. Stoneboro wanted me to and I really liked her. At the church day camp, I learned about God. I had kind of forgotten there was a God. I'd only gone to church once when I was little.

I met Grace at church day camp. I also met Caitlin, Gwen, Timothy, and Jude. On the first day, Gwen, Caitlin, and I thought Jude was a fox. He was the Junior High youth group leader. It's also where I met Abraham, the main youth pastor.

Grace was a year ahead of me in school and lived around the corner. I don't know why we hit it off. We were complete opposites. She lived with both parents and had gone to church her whole life. We had nothing in common, but that was okay.

The first time I spent the night at her house, I had a nightmare. When she woke me up, I told her my dad did "sex things" to me. I don't know why I told her. She wasn't freaked out or anything. I'm not sure she really understood because she was so innocent. She was really comforting and told me it was okay. It wasn't okay, and never would be okay, but she tried to make me feel better.

Grace had six people in her family: Mom, Dad, Charity, Saul, Mercy, and herself. Her dad only had one hand because the other one had gotten blown off in an accident. He worked at a government job and her mom taught nursing at the community college. They were pretty awesome. They let me stay over at their house all the time.

Last summer, after seventh grade, they took me with them to family camp at Mount Hermon for a week. It was really fun. Charity is really a loner. She stays in her room all the time. I sometimes wonder what her deal is. She wears polyester pants and turtle neck shirts every single day, but she is okay, I guess. Saul is cute. He is two years older than Grace. Mercy is a year younger. She is a pain in the butt sometimes, in a little sister kind of way. I always wanted a little sister, and I really like her. She has the prettiest hair. The whole family plays instruments, and I like listening to them practice.

We've been friends since the day we met at church day camp. Grace has never let me down, although I am sure I have let her down. She sticks by me no matter what. I go to church as often as I can, mostly for Grace, because it makes her happy, but I am also friends with Gwen and Caitlin too. Caitlin and Grace hate each other. I wish they didn't. It makes it hard for me because I feel torn between the two of them. Both of them want me all to themselves, and I just want to be friends with both of them.

In Junior High, Grace didn't have many friends. She was kind of a geek. Like she is super smart and likes to read and she plays instruments. Kids are so stupid to think that makes someone weird. That crap never mattered to me anyway. I like her for who she is. She doesn't try to fit in. She's just herself.

One day, these eighth-grade girls were teasing me because I wore the same pair of pants so often. Suddenly, quiet Grace yelled at them to stop. They kept teasing me and then they started in on Grace too. She threw all of her books at them and just exploded. They must not have expected that from her because they backed off and never teased me again. It was really cool that she stuck up for me.

We didn't spend so much time together last year because she started high school, and I was still at LC Junior High. We both got new friends. But she is and always will be my best friend, no matter what happens. It is so cool to have someone who loves me that much.

August 31
Dear Diary,

Only a week left before school starts. I am kinda scared to go to high school. I already have such a bad reputation. I wonder if it will follow me. So what if it does - I don't care. No one understands anyway.

I wish I hadn't slept with Reid - things are so weird now. He wants to be around me all the time, but I really don't want anything to do with him. He really is a loser, 19, living above someone's garage, and partying all the time. "That's where I want to be when I grow up!" she says, dripping with sarcasm. Daphne has such loser friends. She is such a loser herself. Every time mom is gone, all she does is throw parties and make me clean everyone's mess up. Then she yells at me for drinking and doing drugs when she is the one that got me started! "I never did drugs when I was your age." Well, duh, you didn't have an older sister taking you to parties when you were ten, pushing drinks on you, and thinking it was funny. Let's see, my first beer, well besides dad giving it to me - 5th grade, my first pot - 5th grade, cocaine - Daphne and her stupid idiot friends shoving it in my mouth to see what would happen when I was - let's see - oh yeah - 11. It's real hard to figure out why I started at such a young age. How stupid can you be? God - why can't I have a normal family?

No wonder Timothy dumped me. His parents must have been so freaked out that he was dating the "bad" girl. I know I'm young, but I really love him. I wish he knew. I try so hard to do what's right. I can't though, I just can't. I guess the last straw was when I cut myself. He came over to be with me. I think his parents made him break up with me. I wish I was dead. I can't even kill myself right. At least if I was dead, I wouldn't hurt, wouldn't have nightmares. No one would care anyway. Well - maybe a couple of people would.

Love is a Feeling

Love is a feeling you get when you are with someone. I can't describe it, but I know when it happens. Love isn't planned; it just happens. If there were no love, what would this world be like?

You may say it's puppy love, but no one knows for sure. There are many kinds of love and many stages to go through. Each stage brings forth more intimate and deep feelings.

Love doesn't have to be at first sight. You can be friends with someone for years and WHAMO: you're head over heels in love.

Love is the most wonderful feeling in the world. But don't get discouraged because you are ninety-nine and have never been in love –

there is always time.

Timothy

This summer, Timothy and I started to date. His parents never liked me. I don't really know why. I was always polite to them. I guess it might have to do with the fact that my mom doesn't go to church and my parents are divorced. I really like Timothy. He sees past all of the crap. Actually, I love Timothy, but that is a different matter. We had a pretty good summer, but it sucked that his mom always had to drive him to my house. I like being his girl at church. It took him forever to kiss me, but I like just holding his hand and being close to him.

I didn't get to see him as much as I wanted over the summer, but we talked on the phone a lot. Timothy is so different from all the other boys I have known. He could care less about getting down my pants. He says he likes who I am inside. It's beyond me why he likes what he sees, but he does. The only thing is, I feel like I can't really be myself. I have to be this Goody Two-shoes. It's kind of sucky, but I want to be the person he sees, not the person I really am inside. I think there must be a nice person down there somewhere. If not, how could he see it?

Last year during Maranatha, I know he thought I was just a little kid. He was in high school and I was still in eighth grade. I'm really small for my age, so people think I'm younger anyway. I'm not sure what changed. I guess after we started talking some at church he realized I was older than he thought and I always liked talking to him. So, things were good for a while anyway after we started dating. But still, I can't escape feeling like crap all the time.

I don't know what made me do it, but one day I was cleaning the house like I always had to do. I've cleaned the whole house since forever. Daphne is supposed to do half, but she never does, and I just don't want the hassle from mom, so I do it all. So, this one day, about a week before summer ended, I had just finished the whole house and was cleaning mom's bathroom. I was pissed off that I had to clean her bathroom. Why couldn't she clean her own damn bathroom?

There I was, sitting on the floor, getting a new roll of toilet paper from under the sink. I noticed a snakebite kit in the cabinet. I pulled it out and opened it up. There was a razor blade in the kit. Without thinking, I pulled the razor out and started cutting my arms. It didn't even hurt, which surprised me. I liked watching the blood drip all over the sparkling clean floor. I thought about how pissed off mom would be to find me in a pool of blood all over her clean bathroom. She wouldn't be mad about me being dead, just that she had a mess to clean up. I cut both arms on both sides, all the way up and down my forearms. I guess I got scared when I saw how much blood there was.

I called Timothy and asked him to come over. His mom said he couldn't. I told him what I did and that I was scared. Then I told him I was sorry. I apologized again and then hung up. I went back in the bathroom and cut myself more. It didn't matter. He couldn't come, and I wasn't worth his love anyway. I wasn't cutting myself now to see if I could feel pain; I wanted to hurt myself.

I don't really remember what happened, but the next thing I knew, Timothy was in mom's bathroom. He cleaned me up and, I guess, he cleaned up the blood too. I hadn't cut too deeply, or else I probably would have been dead. Timothy bandaged the worst cuts. I kept crying and telling him I was sorry. I didn't know why I did it.

He broke up with me the next day. I think his mom made him, but I'm not sure. It didn't really seem like he wanted to, but maybe that is just me wishing that he still wanted me.

That was the beginning of cutting myself. I wanted to see if I was capable of feeling anything. It never hurt, but in some weird way, it always made me feel more human. I guess just the fact that I could bleed was some sort of twisted comfort. Watching the blood drip made me realize that I was human, even though I didn't feel anything anymore.

Timothy doesn't really even talk to me anymore, not even at church. It really sucks, because, besides Grace, he was the only one who understood. Now I don't even have him for a friend. Maybe someday.

Timmy

I tried to write a poem,
But I couldn't find the words to say.
I want to say I love you,
But I couldn't find a way.

Dear Timmy, where would I be without you?
You cared so much for me.
I love you with all my heart,
You helped make me what I want to be.

So I thought I'd try a song,
Written lovingly to you from me,
To express my utmost feelings of love,
And hope that you can see.

Dear Timmy, where would I be without you?
You cared so much for me.
I love you with all my heart,
You helped make me what I want to be.

I have dreams of us together always,
But I'll leave the planning up to the Lord,
He knows what is best for us,
He will help us cross this ford.

Dear Timmy, where would I be without you?
You cared so much for me.
I love you with all my heart,
You helped make me what I want to be.

You've done so much for me,
Now it's my turn to do something for you.
I'll let you go so you can be happy,
Because Timmy – I love you.

PART 2

Fall

September 3
Dear Diary,

Well, the first day of high school is over. My classes were okay. Same old stuck up jerks though. Even if I wanted to change, they wouldn't let me . . . I would always be the slut and party girl. Even before I was a slut . . .

It's all just the same old crap. There are a couple of good things though. I have choir which is fun. Sarah's dad is my PE coach. Grace and Oskar are here. Timothy is too, but he won't even look at me. Daphne is not here. Other than that, school is going to suck. But at least I don't have to be home when I am at school.

September 5
Dear Diary,

Got drunk before school today. I guess it will be just like 8th grade - drinking to start the day, getting high at lunch. BHS is the same dumb crap as LC Junior High, there are just more jerks to deal with.

I like my chorus class. I am also the aide for the chorus & band teacher, Mr. Meddows. He seems nice. There are a bunch of seniors the hour I aide. A couple of them said hi. One guy Eddy, seems really nice. There's a girl named Amy who seems nice. The other guy, Drew, God -what a fox! But, I shouldn't even think about him - way out of my league. He is Mr. All American and I'm just a slut. He would never even look at me.

I saw Timothy with his new girlfriend today. I felt so freaking stupid when he saw me watching him kiss her. She is absolutely gorgeous. I hope he is happy. At least he has someone that he can be proud of now. She is so much better than I am or ever could be. I don't know what he ever saw in me in the first place. I'm nothing but a loser.

I can't believe Grace would want to stay friends with me. I can't believe her parents let her be friends with me. They know what kind of kid I am. I'm glad they let me hang out over there though. If it wasn't for them, I wouldn't eat half of the time. I like how they all pray as a family and do the Bible study thing. That is cool. I wish my family was a family. Oh well. Life just sucks anyway. You're born, life sucks, then you die. What's the point?

Hello, God? Is there a point to all this suffering? Are you even there? I don't think so anymore.

September 8
Dear Diary,

BHS is okay I guess. Teachers already don't like me because they had my sister . . . nothing like being judged on someone else. At least I won't have to do much to live up to their non-expectations. I go to Grace's house every morning. Her mom makes the best breakfast. It is awesome. I love the way she cooks eggs and tells us all to have a good day. Grace and I walk to and from school together. We don't have any of the same classes because she is a sophomore, but that's all right.

Being a freshman isn't so bad. The first day of school I almost got thrown in a trash can, but some of Daphne's friends stopped them. After that, the older kids left me alone because they figured out I had friends. Also, Daphne's stoner friends look out for me. She doesn't go there anymore because she graduated last year. I'm so glad; I would hate to go to school with her, but it is cool that her loser friends stick up for me.

My favorite part of school is the quad. Everyone hangs out there between classes and at lunch. As a freshman, the only place I am not supposed to go, the senior steps, I can because I know some seniors. Every morning, Andrea and I see each other across the quad and run and give each other big hugs. People look at us like we are whacked, but that is okay. Sarah's dad is the PE coach. He is nice to me because of all the times we went to soccer matches and all of Sarah's swim meets I went to. Sarah and I hardly talk. We are in different groups. She is in the smart, athletic group; I am in the stoner group. But she is not stuck up to me. She is always nice and it's cool that we don't hang out.

My best classes are choir, aide, and German. I never go to my classes, but those are my favorite. The only thing I hate about German class is that my name is Brunhilde. Why? Because I am last in the alphabet and all the good names were picked. Grace is a year ahead in German and we practice talking to each other in

German. She helps me with my homework. She is so smart. She doesn't even have to try, she just gets it all.

  I hate PE, except for coach. I have it first hour so I am gross all day. Even though we have to take showers, there is no time to fix my hair or anything and I hate that. I am still a shrimp and I don't have any boobs. I haven't even started my period yet. I look like a little kid, but I feel like an old lady.

  I like my English class, even though the teacher is like 100 and cranky all the time. We read Steinbeck, and I have been to Cannery Row so that is cool. Some of the kids are so stupid; they don't get any of the books we read. I hate when we have to read aloud in class - it is torture. Most of the kids can't do it right. They stumble over the words and butcher the pronunciation. It is so aggravating. I got picked to read Juliet from Romeo and Juliet because I read well. I love that play and I love Shakespeare. I don't see how the kids don't understand what is going on in the play. It is so easy. Next semester I get to take a mythology class. That will be awesome. I love to read. That is one thing Grace and I have in common. We both read all the time.

Andrea

I met Andrea in eighth grade, and we immediately became friends. Her boyfriend, Shawn, is Stefan's best friend, so we all hang out together. She is absolutely beautiful. I so wish I was that pretty. She lives with her mom and brother. Her parents are divorced, just like mine. Her mom is totally cool. When Andrea started seeing Shawn seriously, her mom took her to get birth control. Her mom talks to her about everything, and they have an awesome relationship.

Andrea is one of the few people who knows about my dad. A little, anyway. It's really hard to tell people, especially since I've had supposed friends screw me over before. Andrea is awesome. We get along about everything, and she isn't jealous of my being friends with anyone else, which is cool, because I always felt like I had to choose one friend over the other with Grace and Caitlin.

She totally understands about my mom too. She knows what a b**** my mom is because she has seen her in action. She always tries to protect me from the mean girls at school and tries not to let me get too messed up when we party. The first time I dropped acid, she was spending the night. We were in my room, and I was looking in the mirror. Suddenly, my face started melting off, and I started to freak out. Andrea held my hand and told me it was just the acid and that I would be okay. She held my face and made me feel that it was still where it was supposed to be so I would stop freaking out. I don't know why I ever took acid again after that happened, but I did. Just stupid, I guess.

Now that we are in high school, we don't have any of the same classes, but we see each other every day before school and at lunch. We usually hang out after school, either at her house or she comes to my house, and we hang out with the guys. Shawn and Andrea are so cute together. Sometimes I hate them both because they are happy, then I feel like a jerk because I love Andrea and only want the best for her. But it sucks so bad when she asks if she can use my room and she and Shawn go to my bed and make love. I should be the one in my bed having sex with someone who loves me. I guess I am just jealous because I know no one will ever love me like that. But I don't feel too bad because I love Andrea and I want her to be happy. It's weird to be happy and jealous at the same time and it makes me feel like a jerk.

September 13
Dear Diary,

The big 14. BFD! The day started out okay. When I got to school, Grace had decorated my locker like a big present. That was neat.

Mom got me a pretty star sapphire necklace and we went out to dinner and I had steak and a baked potato. Why can't I just be happy about the good things? All I can think about is killing myself. Just like last year in Hawaii. All I wanted to do was walk out into the ocean and drown. If I didn't slice my foot open on the glass when I was walking down to the water - I may have just done it. I am so depressed all the time. What the hell is wrong with me? I need to get high. Then I will feel better. The only time life seems worthwhile is if I get high. Maybe that's why I feel so bad, I haven't gotten drunk or high for so long - since last week I guess. Trying to be a goody-two-shoes so Drew All-American will notice me. He is soooo cute - I just melt when I see him. If I didn't have a chance with Timothy - why would I think I would have a chance with Drew? Well, I'm gonna go get wasted at Stefan's now. He always has some good stuff. Then I will feel better.

Stefan

Stefan's my next-door neighbor. His parents are weird, I mean, really weird. He has two older brothers. The oldest is okay. He parties, but he's not a jerk. The middle brother, Damien, is a total creeper. He is always dirty and never showers or brushes his teeth. All he does is get high. He doesn't work—just lives off his parents. I would kick his lazy butt right out of the house. They have lived in their house as long as Stefan can remember. That must be nice: to live in one house all your life.

Stefan is awesome. He is really cute, but more than that, he is just laid-back. He doesn't go around telling secrets or talking about people. The only thing I don't like about him is he is kind of a jerk toward me around the guys, but only sometimes. It's hard being the only girl hanging out with a bunch of guys. But they are all right most of the time. Stefan's a freshman too. The funny thing is, we have gone to school together for three years, but we don't hang out at school, only in the neighborhood. But that's cool. It's not like he totally ignores me at school or anything. We just hang out with different people.

I think I was smoking pot before Stefan. But he has been around it as long as I have because of his brothers. I don't think they forced him to do anything though, like Daphne and her stupid friends did to me. It's a lot easier to force a shrimpy little kid to do something. Because of his older brothers, he always knows where to get the best stuff. I have no idea where he gets money for pot, but he always has some and always shares.

I have been babysitting since fifth grade, so I usually have money. Last summer, I got a job babysitting two kids. I worked all summer, and now I go after school three days a week. I don't get high when I am babysitting.

One day, I was cleaning the house for the parents, and I found their stash of pot. I was so disgusted to discover that they smoke pot. They are supposed to be grownups. Sometimes I don't understand myself. I smoke pot, but they shouldn't? Well, no, they shouldn't. They have responsibilities. I will not party or smoke pot when I have kids. There are a lot of things I won't do when I have kids, like beat the crap out of them, or yell at them, or leave them home alone, or tell them they were a mistake.

Back to Stefan: he has a great room. Most guys plaster their walls with half-naked pictures of Farrah Fawcett. Not him. He has cool black-light pictures. He has a huge boa constrictor. He lets the snake out when we smoke pot. It goes behind the speaker and stretches out up and over the top, pressing itself against the wood. I think it likes the beat from the music. I like how its skin feels really cool and smooth.

Stefan lets me feed it mice when I am there on feeding days. At first, the mice are all scared and hide in the corner. The snake—we just call it Snake because it has no name—ignores the mouse. Once the mouse feels comfortable, Snake goes up to it and flicks its tongue around, then the mouse gets scared again and tries to climb the glass walls. Snake acts bored and moves away. Sometimes, Snake plays this little game with the mouse for hours.

Once the mouse is not afraid anymore, quick as lightning, Snake grabs hold and starts squeezing. Blood pours out of the mouse's mouth. I can hear the bones crunching. The mouse squeals, then it is silent. It is actually really gross but fascinating at the same time.

    I like going to Stefan's house. Even though his parents are nut cases, they leave us alone. I feel sorry for them in a way, but they allowed the boys to do whatever they wanted. Stefan's mom doesn't work, and his dad is always at work. When he comes home, they just sit on the couch, glued to the TV, with drinks in their hands. They don't pay any attention to the kids. One time, Stefan told me that his mom told Damien, "I don't care anymore. There is nothing I can do about you, so do whatever you want." That attitude carried over to Stefan. She just lets him do whatever, and he does. Maybe if I had a son like Damien, I would give up too.

September 15

Dear Diary,

　　Went to youth group tonight. I had to sneak out again to go. I can't believe Mom won't let me go to church. How stupid is that? Most parents would be glad to have their kid go to church. I just don't get it.

　　Everyone sang happy birthday to me. Timothy had his girlfriend with him. It's so hard to look at him. Seeing him with her made the whole night suck. I wish she wouldn't have been there. Why can't I just be happy for Timothy? He deserves someone better than me. I should just be glad he is happy.

　　After church Jude took everyone home. He always takes me home last because I don't want to go home. Gwen, Caitlin, and I are last, in that order. He told me he wanted to give me a birthday present. He kissed me, real kissed me, not a birthday peck on the cheek. That was weird; he's like 24 and has a fiancé, Liliana, the goody-goody church girl. I'm not quite sure how I feel about it. He is really cute, but why would he want to kiss a 14-year-old? He thinks I'm pretty; at least that is what he said.

Church

I've only gone to church for a couple of years, on and off. I have tried to go ever since I went to day camp. It's really hard because I am not sure what to believe. I like the people there, especially Abraham. He can always make me smile, well, almost always. The thing is, most of the time I feel like such a loser because I party all the time then go to church. I even go to church wasted sometimes.

Mom won't let me go to church most of the time. I don't know what her problem is. When I first started going, she was okay with it, but then she told me I couldn't go anymore. She told me she would take me to church one Sunday. I asked her where, and she told me the Church of Satan. She was completely serious. What the hell is that all about! She would rather have me go to a Satanic church? Whatever, man. I so totally don't get her.

I have to sneak out to go to church. Abraham told me that sometimes we have to disobey the world (translation: my parents) if we are obeying God. So, I go to church even though I've been forbidden. Not that she would know anyway. She's never home.

The high school group is pretty fun. We go to someone's house after the church service and play games and eat snacks. We also have a room upstairs at the church with couches and games. It is pretty comfortable. I like hanging out in the youth group room.

Jude and Liliana are the youth group leaders. That's kind of weird, but it doesn't seem to bother Jude in the least. I don't really understand what he is about. How can you teach about God and doing right when you cheat on your fiancé? But there is a certain danger about the whole thing that makes it interesting. I wonder how far he will take it. I wonder how far I want him to take it. I have had a crush on him forever because he is the cute, older guy, but now that he's kissed me, things are so weird. I know what I feel is nothing more than a crush, and there is no danger of feelings getting involved. I just don't know what his game is.

As far as regular church service goes, I like it for the most part. I'm pretty sure I'm going to hell though. I'm just not good enough. I know they say it is not how good you are, it is the trying that matters, but I don't try hard enough. Anyone who tried hard enough would not go to church high. Once, when we were playing hide-and-seek at church, I got high. There is a wall that surrounds the church property and I sat on top of it, hidden in the trees, and smoked a joint. It seems like I can go for a few weeks or a month without getting wasted, but then I just start up with my old habits again. It is too hard to face all the crap in my life without something to help.

September 24
Dear Diary,

   Went to JS elementary school tonight and had sex on the lawn with Doran. I told him I was a virgin. He didn't believe me, but I insisted I was. Why would I say that? I'm not supposed to care. I don't even understand why I had sex with him. I don't even like him - he is a major jerk. Last week we were all high and I didn't walk where he wanted me to, so he almost hit me - right in front of everyone. Oskar was so pissed - he said if he ever caught him hitting me he would beat the living crap out of him. I was glad Oskar stuck up for me. He is so sweet. He is a good friend. Anyway - why I would want to have sex with someone like that is totally beyond me. I am so stupid sometimes that I amaze myself.

Oskar

Oskar is a year older than me. Troy introduced him to the group the year before last when they were both freshmen and I was still in eighth grade. At first, Stefan teased him, calling him Oscar Meyer wiener. I thought Stefan was a jerk for that. But after a while, Oskar just became a part of the group. His dad is from Germany, and that's why he is named Oskar. He is way nice. He has an older brother, Wilhelm, who is a stuck-up jerk. He looks at me like I'm trash whenever I am at Oskar's house. He doesn't even know me, but maybe he knows Daphne and didn't like her. I hate when people don't like me even when they don't know me.

Out of all of the guys, Oskar is my favorite. Sometimes, after we get high and everyone else has gone home, Oskar and I talk. We talk for hours. We talk about everything – school, church, our friends, drugs, the meaning of life. I love the way he thinks about things. He is not dumb. He will go somewhere in his life—not like the rest of the losers around here. Oskar and I will both make something of ourselves, and we won't be stoners forever.

We tried to be boyfriend and girlfriend for a while, but it didn't really work. We like each other as friends better. He hates Doran, and told me I shouldn't go out with him. He was so mad when Doran almost hit me. He said I deserve better. He's right; I won't go out with him anymore. Whenever the guys tease me too much, he tells them to back off.

I love to just sit in my room with him and hang out listening to Pink Floyd. We don't even have to talk. Just being together is awesome. Sometimes, lying together on my bed, we have these really deep conversations about the meaning of life and stuff. He thinks that when I grow up and get away from my mom, I will be okay. I asked him why he gets high, and he said he doesn't even hardly get high. He usually just passes the joint on to the next person, but we are all so wasted, we never notice. That's funny. Here I thought the pot was making him all philosophical and stuff, but he is just that way normally. I really like hanging out with him.

At school, he always comes over to say hi to me, which is cool because he makes an extra effort. Sometimes, when he knows I'm having a bad day, he will just meet me after my classes to check up on me. He's very sweet. Sometimes I wish I could love him like a boyfriend, but I think it would ruin everything.

September 26
Dear Diary,

   I went to a party at Troy's last night. There were tons of people there. By around 1am almost everyone was gone except the usual group. There was only a little Jack Daniels left and Troy said whoever guessed the name of the song would get it. I shouted out "Breakfast in America" by Supertramp and won the last bit in the bottle. I don't know how I knew the group or the song. I never know music stuff and the guys always tease me about not knowing the names of bands or singers.

   Anyway, I was totally wasted already and that put me over the edge. Oskar took me to Troy's room to lie down. I wanted to make out. He is so nice. He told me that he wouldn't make out with me when I was wasted because it wasn't right. I kept asking him to please kiss me because I wanted him to know how much I liked him.

   All of a sudden, I knew I was going to be sick. I ran to the bathroom just in time. As I puked my guts up, Oskar held my hair back. When I was done, he washed my face and took me back to bed. I kept apologizing for throwing up. He kissed me on the forehead and told me not to worry about it and just go to sleep. I woke up with him next to me and we both had all of our clothes on. When he woke up, I thanked him for helping me and caring enough not to take advantage of me. He told me that is what friends are for. He is awesome.

   I am still surprised that I knew the song. But I really could have done without that last drink. If you asked someone who knew me, they would say that my theme song should be "Sex & Drugs & and Rock 'n' Roll" by Ian Dury and the Blockheads. I know that's how I look from the outside, but that's not really what is inside. I think Oskar knows that.

September 28
Dear Diary,

Went to church again and Jude drove me home. After we dropped Caitlin off, he asked if I wanted to talk about the kiss. I told him I didn't understand why he would want to kiss me when he already has a fiancé that is so obviously in love with him. He told me that he thinks I'm totally cool and that if he could break up with her, he would. But his family has known her family since they were little kids. They have been engaged like forever because their families arranged for it. She loves him, but he doesn't really love her. He feels like he has to marry her because his mom is sick and it is her dying wish to see them married. He told me that is the only thing his mom ever wanted from him and he didn't want to disappoint her. That would suck, being forced to marry someone you didn't love. No wonder Liliana loves him though. He is really fine. He kissed me goodbye again. This time, the kiss was a little longer. He asked me not to tell anyone, not even Gwen or Caitlin.

Caitlin and Gwen

Caitlin and Gwen are both freshmen, just like me. I have known them since Day Camp, when I met Grace. I really like them both, and since we are all in the same grade, we hang around together. Caitlin doesn't like that I smoke pot—she doesn't know the half of it—but Gwen doesn't really care. Both of them have great houses and basically whatever they want or need.

Caitlin's dad died when she was little. Her mom is remarried, and her stepdad is okay. She doesn't have problems with him. I like to stay at her house, but she lives in San Jose now, so it's pretty far to go. The weird thing is, she lives pretty close to Elise. Sometimes when I go see Caitlin, I also go see Elise. Even though Caitlin's mom and dad go to a church in San Jose, they let Caitlin come to church here because this is where she grew up and all her friends are here. Next year, she has to go to her parent's church. She said she likes the youth group there and that she will miss our church but she wants church friends at her new school. That makes sense, but I will miss her when she leaves. It seems like this year we are growing apart, and Gwen and I are getting somewhat closer.

Gwen doesn't come to youth group a lot these days. She is out partying. Her parents are getting divorced, and it kind of screwed her up. So, our little group is growing apart, but when we are together, it is still great. I guess I am part of the problem of growing apart because I have this big secret about Jude. It's weird not telling anybody about him, but I don't. I am good at keeping secrets. Daddy taught me well.

October 5
Dear Diary,

    I haven't written for a while. I ran away from home. I went to Andrea's house. Her mom is so cool. She called my mom and asked if I could just hang out there for a while. Mom was probably glad to get rid of me, after all, she reminds me that I was an accident every chance she gets. I don't know why she just didn't give me away when I was born. I would have been better off anyway!

    When I finally talked to her on the phone after a week of being at Andrea's house - she asked me what was wrong. I told her she doesn't even know me or care about me; she said she did. I told her that I did drugs all the time, including LSD and that I wasn't a virgin. I told her she is never home and she has no idea about anything in my life. She didn't even say anything to me except for "oh." Care? Yeah right! She doesn't give a crap about me. If she cared, maybe she would stay home once in a while. She is never home. She is always out screwing some guy - including her married boss! Everyone in the neighborhood talks about her. She is such a slut. No wonder I am a slut - such great role models that I have in my life.

    I wish when I got taken from her and put in the children's shelter they would have kept me. I begged and begged to go to a foster home, but they wouldn't let me. I liked staying at the shelter so much better. At least it was safe. The school there was fun and I liked being around all the little kids. I felt sorry for them though. All of them lived in the same kind of crap I do - it made me feel, well, sorta normal.

    The shelter should have kept me, knowing that my mom was going to make me stay with my dad so she could go play on the beach in freaking Acapulco!!!! She knows what dad did to me. Maybe she still doesn't believe me. Stupid idiot - make me go to a stupid hypnotist when I finally got up the nerve to tell her that dad was having sex with me. That was the hardest thing I ever had to do - and then she wouldn't even believe me. I had to go talk to that weirdo so she could see if I was telling the truth. Like I would make something like that up. God - didn't she ever wonder why I would get sick every time I had to go over there? And then my dad - what a piece of work. Princess my foot. More like sex toy. Always telling me how much he loved me. Selfish jerk! After all that - the jerk only went to jail for a couple of freaking months - and the witch was sending me to stay with him so he could rape me again! Selfish slut, witch, whore!

Children's Shelter

When I was in sixth grade, Morgan and I were good friends. We always hung out at her house after school. She had this huge tree that we would climb and sit in. I guess it reminded me of the trees in the mountains. One time, we decided to get high up there. I remember we started laughing, and I fell out of the tree. It was funny, but if I got hurt it probably wouldn't have been so funny.

I told her about my dad because I thought I could trust her. We had even made a blood-sister pact. Toward the end of the year, we got into a fight about something stupid, and she said she was going to tell everybody that my dad had sex with me. I guess I was already upset because I knew in a few weeks I would have to stay with him while my mom was in Acapulco. I remember the day so clearly.

I went to the teacher's lounge at lunch, which was unheard of. No one knocked on that door! I was crying and asked for Mrs. Molere. She came out, and I told her that Morgan was going to tell my secret. I didn't want to tell her what it was because I was embarrassed. I thought that if she knew, she wouldn't like me anymore. She sat down on the wall next to me. She talked to me gently and told me I needed to tell her or she couldn't do anything about it. What I didn't know was that Morgan was already telling everyone while I was talking to Mrs. Molere.

I guess I was really scared. I opened my mouth and everything started spilling out. I told her a little about my dad and what he had been doing to me my whole life and that I hadn't seen him overnight for a year, but now my mom was sending me to stay with him for two whole weeks. I was shaking so badly as I told her. After telling my mom and not being believed, it was so scary to tell an adult. You should have seen her face. I felt really awful for telling her and making her have that horrified look on her face. I hardly even told her anything, but she was still shocked at what I was telling her. Maybe it really was bad.

Thinking back, I am sure that she had no idea my secret would have been about my dad having sex with me. Things like that just were not talked about. I didn't know anyone who was even hit by their parents, let alone all the stuff I told her. She was pregnant, and it really bothered me that I had upset her. She told me not to worry and that she would take care of me. I was really hoping she would just let me stay with her during the time my mom would be gone.

Later that day, I saw her talking to Morgan, which didn't really help because she had already blabbed. I think most people thought she was lying anyway. When we were in line, waiting to go back in to class, one of the boys said; "You had sex with your dad. You're a slut!" I gave him the meanest look I could and said, "Yeah, it happened. So what? You don't know anything. If you say one more thing, it'll be the last thing you ever say!" He was one of those kids that backed down as soon as someone talked back. The rest of the kids left me alone after that. My friend Sarah was really nice about knowing. She didn't ask me about it all mean and stuff. She asked me if I was okay. She said I could stay at her house while my mom was gone.

The day after I told Mrs. Molere, I was at home after school, and two grown-ups knocked on the door, a man and a woman. Mom wasn't home. They told me that they were there to take me away. I told them no, I wasn't going anywhere, and I slammed the door. I would not reopen it. They finally went away. I didn't tell anyone about them.

The next day, I was at Sarah's swim meet counting laps for her. The man and woman came to the swim meet. My stomach felt like lead. I got so scared. I don't know how they found me there. They told me that they had talked to my mom and she'd said it was okay for me to go with them. When I asked where they were taking me, they said a home for kids. I asked why, and they said so I wouldn't have to stay with my dad when my mom was gone. When I asked them how they knew, they told me Mrs. Molere was worried about me and asked them to come talk to me. Sarah's dad said I should go with them. Since it was Saturday, I couldn't go to school to ask Mrs. Molere if she had sent them, but I decided that if that was how she was helping me, I would go. It was better than going to my dad's house anyway.

When we got to the shelter, there were several big rooms. They put me in a room with the littler kids. It was all colorful with a bunch of beds in the room, all placed around a circle. Each bed had its own little space for stuff. Of course, I didn't have anything, not even my teddy bear. I was a little scared. But then the owners, or whoever they were, brought me into a room and had me pick out new clothes, anything I wanted to wear. That was kind of fun. The only new clothes I'd had for years were the ones I'd bought with my own money or had stolen because I had no money for clothes. I ate dinner, took a shower, and then went to bed. It was weird sleeping there, especially without my teddy. I didn't get much sleep. One little girl, about five, was crying, so I went and crawled into bed with her, and both of us finally fell asleep.

The next morning, they woke us up at seven, and we went to breakfast. The kids all went to school, but I was taken to a room with the people who had picked me up and a cop named William. I was scared at first because I thought I'd done something wrong. I thought for sure they were going to take me to juvie. I knew what happened to kids who went to juvenile hall, and I didn't want to go there. I was really scared. The cop told me that they just wanted to ask some questions. I wasn't in trouble, and I wasn't going to juvie. I calmed down a little bit.

They asked me a lot of questions about home and my dad. I didn't tell them everything, like about the parties and stuff, but I did tell them that my mom was never home and some things about my dad. That was really scary because I'd never told anyone everything about him before, not even my mom—not after her reaction and everything. I just held everything inside. I didn't even tell Mrs. Molere everything, just that my dad did bad sex things to me. Well, maybe I told that hypnotist guy. I really don't remember what happened there.

William told me to call him by his first name because he was there to help me and he wasn't a cop right then. That was cool. He had drawings of a man and a child, both naked. He made me point on the pictures to the places I was talking about when I explained what my dad did to me. If he didn't understand something, he would ask me to explain again.

I was so scared. I was shaking so hard that they brought me a blanket. I felt like I was going to throw up. My dad always told me not to tell because something terrible would happen to my brother, sister, or my mom and that everyone would think I was a lying little slut. I just knew that my dad would kill my brother and sister when he found out that I had told his secret. Oh, my God. What was I doing telling these people?

Nothing would change, and I was going to be in huge trouble. I was also worried that my mom wouldn't know where I was, but the man and woman told me that she knew I was safe and not to worry about it. William tried to reassure me that nothing was my fault and I was not in trouble. It didn't help much. I don't know what made me spill everything I did to these strangers. I think I was more scared of going to my dad's for two whole weeks with no one to protect me than I was of my dad just killing me and getting it over with.

They had a tape recorder, and the two people took notes while William asked questions. I had to use the exact words; penis, vagina, anus, mouth . . . I couldn't just say privates. I had to explain every place he touched me, what he put where, and what he made me do to him. I was so ashamed because I knew what he did was wrong and I should not have let him. I should not have made him do those things to me. It was all because I was such a horrible little girl. William told me that wasn't true, but I didn't believe him. I knew good girls did not do those things with their daddies.

After they had talked to me, they took me to class. That was neat because the school was right there, and the classes only had a few kids in them. It was just about lunchtime, and I was a little hungry. A few days later, William came to get me from class and told me I had to go see a doctor. He didn't tell me why I had to go to the doctor, but he did bring me a teddy bear. Since I missed lunch, he took me to McDonald's. We didn't exactly go to a doctor, but to a hospital. It was horrible. I was so mad at William for not telling me what would happen.

The doctor brought me into this little room with a table. I had to get undressed and put on a gown. He told me to lie on my back with my legs up and my feet on the table. He got this metal thing and shoved it up my vagina without even telling me. I had no idea what was happening. I just went somewhere else in my mind, like I did when my dad was messing with me. When he was done, he told me to go the bathroom, get dressed, and sit on the chair in the hall. When I tried to pee, it hurt like crazy, just like when dad finished with me. I threw up my lunch. I was so scared I couldn't even cry. The only thing missing from the experience was a shower. I felt like I had just been raped by a stranger. It even hurt to sit in the chair. I could not find a comfortable position, and I was so ashamed of what had happened.

When William came to get me, I wouldn't even talk to him. He had broken my trust. I just kept shaking. I hurt so bad from the "examination," but more than that, I had put my trust in this man and he had totally turned his back on me. I think that was worse than what the doctor had done to me.

On the way back to the shelter, William told me he was sorry, but he had to take me to the doctor because they had to see if my dad had hurt me inside. I finally started to cry and told him he could have at least warned me about what would happen. I was expecting a stick down my throat and saying, "Ahh" and not some doctor shoving his fingers and a metal thing up me! William told me he was so sorry and that he didn't really know what to tell me because he had never heard a story as bad as mine before. I believed he was sorry. I felt bad for him. He didn't know how to deal with a screwed-up little kid. I bet he didn't know that he would have to listen to that kind of story when he became a cop. I forgave him.

The next day is burned into my memory forever. My mom was coming to see me after lunch. The whole day I was worried, but I was glad that she was going to come. After lunch, I sat in the big waiting room. There were huge double doors to enter the building and a desk on the right side. The building was circular with rooms all around the perimeter. The middle of the building was the waiting area. It was sunken into the floor with benches built into the wall. I waited across from the entrance so I could see my mom when she came in the door. I waited for almost an hour. Finally, she came.

When I first saw her face, my worst fears were realized. She was pissed off! She came storming up to me without checking in with the lady at the desk. The first words out of her mouth were, "Thanks for ruining my trip to Acapulco! You ruined my entire life! You are the most selfish person ever born! How could you do this to me you stupid little . . .."

The lady at the desk had called someone, and they came to take my mom to another room. I just sat there in shock, not knowing what to do. Why couldn't she understand? Everyone at the shelter was telling me that it wasn't my fault, but with the reaction from my mom, how could I believe them? It had to all be my fault for her to hate me so much.

I begged the teachers and workers at the shelter to keep me there. I told them I would help with all the little kids and I wouldn't be any bother. I begged and begged. I did not want to go home. I was too scared. I didn't want my mom to hate me anymore. I knew if I were not home, she would just forget about me and her life would be so much better. Nothing worked. I knew I was doomed to go back to hell and make my mom's life miserable.

William came to get me for court a few days later. I was scared to go to court. Everyone was so mad at me already. I had a plan for when it was my turn to talk. I would just tell the judge that I was sorry for causing such a mess. I would tell him that I had lied about everything. I didn't know how I could sit there with my mom and dad in the room and tell the truth. I didn't want to be in any more trouble, and I didn't want my dad to hurt my mom, my brother, and my sister. I just wanted everyone to love me. I felt like if I told the judge it had all been a mistake, maybe, just maybe, everything would be okay and I would be loved again.

I remember that I wore a pretty dress. I can't remember the color, just that it was frilly. I also remember the ladies at the shelter had fixed my hair with barrettes and bows. I don't remember my mom ever fixing my hair for me. William said I looked so pretty and not to worry, the judge would be really nice to me. My mom came into the court building and didn't even talk to me. She just gave me a dirty look as she stormed by. At least William saw that! I wanted to cry. Why did she hate me so much? I was afraid of seeing my dad walk by, but he never did. Finally, William told me it was time for him to go into the courtroom and for me to wait right where I was.

I had to sit all by myself in the hall for so long. The bench was hard, and my feet didn't touch the floor, but I was wearing a dress and couldn't pull my feet under me Indian-style. William finally came out of the courtroom and said that the judge wanted to talk to me alone. I did not have to see my dad or mom. Just the judge and William would be there with me.

When I went to the judge's office, he was just a regular guy. I really expected him to be scary. He had a nice voice. He asked me how old I was and if I knew that telling the truth was important. He told me that they had listened to the tape recording of everything I had told William while I was waiting. He asked if the stuff I had told William was true. His voice was so nice and his eyes were so kind, I could not go through with my lie.

I started to say no, but he was looking intently at me, so I told him everything I had told William was true. He thanked me for being so brave. I asked if I had to go and stay with my dad anymore, and he told me that I didn't ever have to see him again. When I asked if my dad was going to jail, the judge said yes.

I started to cry because I had just made my daddy go to jail. William held my hand, and the judge told me that my dad knew what he had done was wrong and he knew he had to go to jail. He also told me my dad was not mad at me. Something about his voice made me believe him.

When we were leaving, I turned around and asked him if I could ask one more question. When he said yes, I said, "Can I stay at the shelter? I don't want to go back home. My mommy hates me." He told me he was very sorry, but

I had to go home with my mom, and he was sure that she loved me.

On the ride back to the shelter, William and I talked. I was glad I didn't have to talk in front of my mom and dad. Court wasn't as scary as I thought it would be. I asked William if there was any way that I didn't have to go home. He said if he could take me home he would, but he couldn't. The law would not allow it. He said, "The judge was right. You are very brave. I have never met anyone braver. I know you don't want to go home, and I understand why. There is nothing anyone can do about it. You just need to be brave some more." He was very nice, and I was glad I forgave him for the doctor thing. Before he dropped me off at the shelter, he bought me a strawberry milkshake.

I'm not sure how long I was at the shelter—at least a few weeks. Every day, I thought about running away so I would not have to go home. I just didn't know where to go. I was only eleven years old.

The morning my mom came to get me was horrible. I got dressed in my own clothes and waited in the same spot where she told me I had ruined her life. Every time I heard a noise, I got scared. William walked in the door. He said he wanted to see me one last time. He told me, "Always remember it wasn't your fault. You are the bravest person I know." He hugged me, and I cried. I asked if he could just adopt me. He said he wished he could. When he let me out of the hug, I saw tears in his eyes. That made me cry harder. He patted my head, walked out the door, and out of my life.

My mom finally got there, two hours after she was supposed to show up. She didn't talk to me the entire way home. She didn't talk or pay any attention to me for months, except to yell at me about something or slap me across the face. I felt horrible, knowing that I caused so many problems. I tried to be extra good so my mom would love me, but she just stayed angry at me all the time. I learned just to stay out of her way and perfectly do everything she asked me to so she wouldn't find fault and slap me upside the head.

October 19

Dear Diary,

   My mom was gone on a trip for a whole week. All Daphne did was party with her friends. I miss David so much. I wish he would come home from boot camp. I can't wait until I will be able to see him at Christmas. Eddy and Amy, they are in Band and are seniors, talked to me today when I was done with my aiding stuff. They told me that I could do whatever I wanted with my life. Can you imagine that? They don't have a clue, good families and all. But it was nice of them . . . they even know I do drugs. They said I could quit whenever I wanted and that I was smart and could get good grades if I tried. They said even with my mom not caring about me, that it was up to me what I did with my life. I guess they see inside of me just like Timothy did. What is it that they see anyway? All I see is a stupid druggie slut that can't keep anything important. No wonder Timothy won't be with me. I wish he knew that I still loved him and that his girlfriend is no way good enough for him. She's so fake. At least I have a reason to be a slut . . . why should I care when I can't even remember ever being a virgin . . . there is no reason to ever try to be one. It is hopeless to try to be pure, because there is no purity or goodness inside of me.

   I'm going to go get high now, then I won't feel or care anymore. The only time I don't hurt is when I am numb from the drugs. This morning my eyes were so black, not even a little brown anymore. Why can't anyone see how much I hurt inside? Everyone knows the eyes are the windows to the soul, so why can't they see my pain?

Spinning Out of Control

Spinning, swirling, storming
Drowning, dangling, dying
Clawing, crying, crawling
Hope is nonexistent, vaporous

Life is a "Why bother" proposition
No matter what, no matter when
It all goes down the drain
Happiness is merely an illusion for the masses

Drag through each day
Fight through each night
Cry with tears that no one sees
Leave the world a better place

Get things in order
Leave no signs
Accidents happen always
No saying goodbye

Disillusioned in love
Tired of life
Sick of the continual pain
No more to suffer in silence

It's over . . . the end

David

David is five years older than me. When mom and dad got divorced, David moved with dad. I think he hated it there. I think dad always beat the crap out of him too. The only thing I like about going to dad's is that I got to see David. I always spend as much time as I can with him. He is my hero. He is quiet and smart, and he loves me to pieces. I like to watch him build things. He can build anything electronic. One time, he made a machine that made birdcalls. It sounded just like the birds in the mountains. It was so funny because we put it by the window and turned it on. All of these little birds came looking for the bird making the song.

Even though I loved to see David, I hated going to my dad's. The days were okay. We would go play goofy-golf, or dad would drop us off at the movies, and we would spend all day there. The nights were the worst.

Dad would call to me, "Princess, come sit with me." No matter how big I got, I had to sit on his lap when we were watching TV. He would always put his hand down my pants. One time I asked him not to do that because I was too big. He slapped my face as hard as he could and told me he was my father and he could do whatever he wanted. A few hours after that, he took me in the kitchen and taught me how to French kiss. I was pretty little, maybe second or third grade. He told me that was his special way to say he was sorry for slapping me. It was just that he loved me so much and always wanted to show me. It hurt his feelings that I pushed him away when he hardly ever got to see me. He told me that from now on that would be our special way of kissing.

After I went to bed, the night he taught me to French kiss, I threw up everywhere. I couldn't get the taste of him out of my mouth. He made David clean up my puke, and then Dad took me to bed. I always had to sleep in his bed. He made me have sex with him right after I was sick to my stomach. Then it was off to the shower with his words about how much he loved me.

So, seeing David was good, but was also always hard because of my dad. When I was in fourth grade, I asked to sleep in David's room. David had bunk beds, and he and Daphne shared the room when we came to visit. I always had to sleep with dad. I thought I would be safe in David's room. I feel asleep on the floor, so happy not to be in my dad's bed. It was the first time I had not willed myself to stay awake in such a long time. The next thing I knew, I woke up to my dad crawling in the sleeping bag on the floor with me. He did me right there, right next to David and Daphne. I felt so sick. I never asked to sleep in there again. I was so ashamed of myself for allowing that to happen.

David is in the Air Force now. He came to live with us after Dad went to jail. Mom hated David living with us. She couldn't wait to get rid of him. So, as soon as he was seventeen, she signed him up for the Air Force. I cried and cried when he left on the bus. Mom just turned around and walked to the car without even watching the bus pull away.

I write him letters, but he is too busy to write to me very much. He hardly ever calls. He probably doesn't want to talk to mom. I can't imagine why! But when he does write, it is to me—not mom, not Daphne—just his baby sister. The thing I love most about him is that I am his baby sister, and he always tries to stick up for me. Even though he is really my half-brother, he has never said that. He always tells his friends, "This is my little sister." He doesn't mind me hanging out with him. I just like to be around him. I really don't think he likes Daphne too much. They don't get along. She doesn't understand him. I miss him a lot and can't wait for Christmas when he can come home on leave. I am very proud of him. He gets good marks in all of his classes and he said he does good in his training. He got some awards already from boot camp. I'm sorry he hates it there, but in a way, it's probably better than being here.

At least he doesn't have to deal with Mom hating him to his face.

October 23
Dear Diary,

   Youth group again tonight. This time Jude frenched me. He asked if it was okay when he was done. I kinda laughed and asked what he meant. He said Liliana won't kiss him because she wants to stay "pure" and he has never frenched anyone before. I'm not sure I believed him. I thought he kissed really good. I'm feeling kinda good that he chose me to fool around with. Does that make sense? God, what a slut! But at least it is fun? What a twisted way of having fun. I don't think I even know what fun is . . . I don't even like him that much, other than the fact that he is cute, but he is a good kisser.

October 31
Dear Diary,

   Halloween . . . I had fun tonight. I got wasted before I went out with my friends. I dressed up as a baby with my footie jammies and my teddy bear. I got so much candy and had a good time just pretending to be a little kid with no cares. I wish people knew how much I pretended.

November 15
Dear Diary,

   I haven't written in a while. Things have been pretty messed up. I have been getting high all the time. The only classes I go to are my aide class, so I can look at Drew, and choir. Other than that, I don't give a damn. My mom has no clue that I never go to school. I come home; she is asleep and doesn't hear me. I get drunk or high and sleep. Then I go out at night and get high some more. Pot doesn't do anything to make my life go away anymore, so I do everything else. LSD, ludes, shrooms, speed, coke, I guess the only drug I haven't done is heroin. All the time I am high, but it doesn't help anymore. My eyes get blacker every day. No one sees or even cares that I am so depressed. I can't have Timothy. I can't have Drew. I am not good enough for anyone. I am not good enough for myself. I hate being me. Even Grace doesn't know how much I hurt inside. God . . . why can't someone see? Is there really even a god?

My Hurt

Is anyone out there?
Can you hear me call?
All this pain I'm going through
Lord, don't let me fall.

Does anybody understand?
Feel what I feel?
Someone tell me please,
Why was this planned?

Please, Lord, won't you help me now?
Show me how to be strong.
Help me to love them, Lord,
Even when they're wrong.

I don't want to hurt anymore.
I just want to walk with you.
Open my eyes, dear Lord,
Walk into my door.

Show me how to have no fear,
Give me the words to say.
I need your courage, Lord,
Help me through my day.

I want to thank you, Lord,
For all the things you've done.
I want to live for you,
To have your sword.

So I just praise your name,
Though things are bad.
Because I know You will get me through,
And make me glad.

Mom

I think my mom never wanted kids. She tells me all the time that I was an accident and that she never wanted any more kids. She pretty much ignores us, except when she is in a bad mood. The only time she is halfway decent is on trips, like on the Hawaii trip. She was okay. It was me that was all screwed up. But how do you live with someone who changes from total witch to nice overnight and then back again in the blink of an eye? It's pretty hard.

My mom was married before she married my dad. She already had David and Daphne when she married my dad. My dad was forty-two when I was born, and she was twenty-five. That's a pretty big age difference. She met him at work. I don't remember a time when they got along. They always fought. My dad had some other kids too, but I only found that out by accident. When I was really little, I answered the phone and some lady said she wanted to talk to RJ. She told me her name, but I forgot it. I said there was no RJ, because I was too little to know my dad's name. I hung up the phone. My dad asked who I was talking to and I told him some lady wanted RJ and said she had the wrong number and hung up. My mom said that was daughter. He told my mom to shut up and he never said anything about his other kids again.

The only really good times growing up were when we went on family vacations with Herbert, Margaret, and their son Harry. I liked going to Lake Tahoe to play in the snow and, right before the divorce, we went to Baja California. Dad always acted like Super Dad on those vacations. We never got yelled at or hit. Most importantly, he never fooled around with me on the family trips. He was just the best dad ever. No one would ever know what a creep he was. But Dad and Mom were always just fine on those trips. What a bunch of lies now that I look back on those days. It was nothing but a big act, but those were the only good times I ever remember in my family, so I hold onto them, even if they were fake.

Ever since the divorce, Mom has been out with more men than I can count. She had a steady boyfriend for about a year right after the divorce. He took us to Pismo Beach, and we rode in his Jeep on the sand dunes. It was really fun. He also took us camping. I had never been camping before. It was so much fun sleeping in a tent, but all Mom did was complain the entire trip. He had a big Irish setter that was really sweet. I liked him. He never looked at me the way my dad did. I never felt scared of him. They broke up though. Since then, it's just been guy after guy.

Right now, it's Jacob. He works with her and lives with us while he works here. He moves from job to job. He goes all over the country, wherever they need him. He is really nice, but the whole thing sucks. Every Sunday, he calls his family and talks to them, telling them how much he loves them and misses them. The rest of the week, he sleeps in her bed. It's weird, but I like him anyway. Maybe his wife isn't nice. He bought me a pretty coat, and he has an airplane and takes us flying. Once we flew to the ocean and had brunch, then flew back. It was fun. My mom usually goes out with married men. I guess she doesn't have to make a commitment that way.

She really is a horrible parent. She is never home, even after I ran away and told her about all of the drugs and stuff. She just doesn't care. She works nights, then on her nights off she is out with her boyfriend of the week. She goes on weeklong trips and leaves me home alone. Daphne is supposed to take care of me, but that doesn't exactly work out. It's more like me taking care of myself. Daphne never stays home when Mom is gone. I don't know where she goes, but she isn't home.

I hate when Mom gets mad. All of a sudden, she just blows up and slaps me across the face. She has these nails that scrape across my face and leave marks. I hate being slapped. I'd rather be beaten with the belt like my dad does. At least people don't see those marks. It's embarrassing to have nail marks streaked across my face. And I never know what sets her off either. She just strikes out for no reason. It really sucks, especially when it is in front of one of my friends. I cannot figure her out.

One day, last summer, she came home and found my friend Genevieve and me in the backyard toking on a homemade bong. She asked what we were doing, and I lamely said, "Experimenting." She told us to throw it away, and then put us both in the car and drove us to the mall. She told us to follow her and not say a word. There we were, high as kites, following her through the mall like naughty little puppies while she shopped. We were there about an hour, wondering when she was going to yell at us. We just kept following her around. She bought some shoes for herself, and then we left for home. She never said a word about the pot. Whatever. I don't get her.

I'll never forget the day I told her about my dad. We were driving to his house for my weekend visit. Daphne wasn't going since she was older and could just go hang out with her friends. I told her I didn't want to go, that I didn't feel good. She said I had to go. I begged and begged. Finally, she started yelling at me. She told me that she never got any time alone and all she wanted was a weekend. I started crying uncontrollably. She yelled, "What the hell is your problem?"

I was trying to talk through my tears, and I told her that dad did stuff to me. She says, "What stuff?" in a really mean voice. I told her, "Bad stuff." She still didn't get it. How freaking stupid can you be? I finally had to spell it out for her, that he was having sex with me.

She was so pissed off. She gave me the dirtiest look ever. She turned the car around right in the middle off the road, squealing the tires. I didn't try to talk to her on the way home. I could tell she was really mad. When we got home, she didn't say a thing to me. She just told me to go to my room and stay there.

I heard her on the phone with my dad, telling him I was sick and wouldn't be coming that weekend. I didn't even get dinner. I just stayed in my room all night wondering why she was so mad at me. My dad must have been right. I had done really bad things to him, and now that my mother knew, she would never love me again.

The next week she took me to a "doctor." He turned out to be a hypnotist. He asked me all kinds of questions at first, telling me that if I lied, he would know. I don't really remember any of it except for a crazy circle thing on the wall and his watch in front of my face. I guess I was out of it. The next thing I remembered was my mom telling me it was time to go home. She was all pissed off again.

I didn't have to see my dad for a while. I don't know what Mom told him. She never talked to me about any of it. I guess it was a big secret or something. It really makes me mad that she didn't believe me when I told her.

Thinking back, there were signs that something was wrong, but she never paid attention. I guess that would have required thinking about someone other than herself. I don't have a lot of respect for her. Even after she knew about my dad, I still had to go with the jerk. Just not for overnights anymore. But it still sucks. The way he looks at me… gross. He likes to take me shopping and have me try on clothes. He always stares at me. I hate it. But I have learned to play games to get what I want. I try on the clothes and parade around in front of him. After we shop, I ask for some money, and I always get it. What a loser idiot. Show some T and A and then I get the money. I feel like a whore when I play him that way, but who the hell cares? At least I get something for all the years of hell he put me through.

Stone Cold

Mama, do you see me cry?
Do you feel my pain?
Do you feel anything?

Mama, you are cold.
I learned hardness from you,
And to run and hide.

Mama, did you ever believe?
You hid your pain from me,
Or did you really just not care?

Mama, how could you send me back?
You are such a selfish witch.
How can you face yourself in the mirror?

Never cry, you told me,
Pull yourself up by your bootstraps,
Don't care—don't feel.

What the hell do you know
With your hard heart
And your selfish ways?

You who should have believed—
You who did not protect—
You with the revolving bedroom door.

What did you teach me?
Hide it all inside,
Be hard, do not cry.

What did I learn from you?
Hold in emotion.
Replace lovers when it gets too close.

I know these things,
Know you taught me wrong,
But how to change . . .
Years of hiding me,
A perfect mask for my less-than-perfect self,
Never showing reality.

What to do now,
When the pain finds my hiding place?
Cry? Reveal? No, never.

Show who I am inside,
Do I even know anymore?
I have hidden for so long.

Always striving for perfection,
To cover up the lies,
I must be better than the rest.

Mama, why can't I cry?
I feel so much pain—
Did you ever feel anything . . .

November 27
Dear Diary,

We had Mexican food for Thanksgiving dinner. It was good, but Daphne and Mom were fighting. It is all they ever do. I hate this family! I want David to come home. One more month.

December 10
Dear Diary,

I went to the Christmas Ball with Matthias. I wasn't going to go, but then he said he arranged with Drew to get a ride. So, slut that I am, I said I would go. I don't like Matthias that way, but I wanted to be with Drew, even if he was with someone else. Genevieve asked her sister Coline if I could borrow her dress from last year. She said yes. I couldn't believe it. It is white with blue velvet. I looked pretty, even Drew said so. I was supposed to be grounded. My mom said I couldn't go to the dance. The stupid idiot went out of town for the weekend with one of her boyfriends. She actually thought I would stay home? What a dumb idiot.

Anyway, we went to this fancy restaurant in Los Gatos. I was really sick and had a fever so I just had some French onion soup. I never had it before, it was really good. I didn't dance too much because I was sick, at least that is what Matthias thought. It was really hard seeing Drew with another girl, but I was happy just being next to him. Drew promised me one dance, and it was a slow dance. Matthias danced with Drew's date.

My heart beat so hard when we danced. I just wanted to melt into him and never wanted that dance to end. I was surprised that Drew picked a slow dance for the promised one. Maybe he does like me but doesn't want to go out with a freshman? He said he liked how I danced and told me thanks. I wonder if Matthias noticed that I was all shaky after dancing with Drew.

After the dance, we drove up the old Highway 9 to the Santa Cruz Mountains. We parked and Drew had some champagne. We all drank some, then Drew and his date went out in the woods. Matthias tried to kiss me - he doesn't know how to kiss at all. He shoved his tongue down my throat and slobbered all over me. Gross! I said I needed some air, so we sat outside. I really just wanted to hear if Drew was screwing his date. They came back to the car a little rumpled, but I don't think they did anything. God, I am such a slut, but I don't care. As long as I can be close to Drew, I will do anything. The one dance was magic and I will hold it close to my heart always. A part of me is so afraid, though. Do I want to love again? I still love Timothy, so why someone new? I need to move on. I need to leave Timothy alone. He deserves so much better than I can ever give.

PART 3

Winter

December 13
Dear Diary,

    I am in Kaiser in the mental ward. I don't care! I'm glad I'm here. Last week, I cut school with Oskar. I was so depressed; I just didn't know what to do anymore. I tried to cut my wrist and he was fighting with me, trying to get the glass away. A cop saw us struggling and after figuring out what happened, he took me to the county hospital. I tried to crawl out of the bathroom window and run away, but he sent a nurse in to check on me. I was halfway out the window when she pulled me back in. Anyway, after my mom came, they told her I had to come here. She was so freaking mad. She yelled at the doctor and told them I was just trying to get attention. So, when will I get some attention? When I'm dead? At all of 14, I'm a hell of a lot smarter than she is. Of course it is a cry for help. Notice me . . . life sucks . . . I hurt! I don't have any damn bootstraps to pull myself up!

    She yelled at me during the entire two-hour drive to the hospital, but I was high so I didn't really care. Well, I did, but she doesn't know. Why is she so mad, why can't she understand? I think I will like it here, I wish I could stay forever. But it will be just like the shelter and they will send me home.

December 14
Dear Diary,

I don't want to go home. They are making my dad come tomorrow. I don't want to see him; doesn't anybody understand that I don't want to go home? I'll just kill myself as soon as I get the chance if they make me go.

There is this guy here, Thomas, he was in Vietnam. He is really screwed up. Last night we were talking, just him and me, he got really upset for some reason and the doctors and nurses came and got him. Great big guys had to wrestle him to the ground. They took him away in a strait jacket. I cried and cried because I made him so sad. I don't even know what I said. The shrink said it wasn't my fault, that Thomas was just messed up from everything he saw in the war. I feel so bad for him. That must suck.

They finally moved my roommate out. All she did was cry every night and I couldn't sleep. Now I am by myself. I like to be by myself; then no one can hear me cry. I'm going to sleep now.

Kaiser Psych Ward

Most people think that being in a mental hospital would be awful. Actually, it's great. I was safe and free of Mom and Daphne for a while. Maybe this time someone would listen and let me go to a foster home.

The actual hospital is really nice, not like you see on One Flew Over the Cuckoo's Nest. It doesn't even look like a hospital, just a bunch of nice buildings. The grounds are pretty with flowers, grass, walking paths, and benches to sit and look at the gardens. The inside is also nice. The rooms are decorated in nice soft colors like yellow, blue, and beige. Patients share a room, and there is a kitchen, a TV room, a game room, and a group meeting room. The doctors have their own offices. The nurses and doctors just wear normal clothes. The patients don't have to wear gowns. We get to wear our own clothes.

I arrived at night, and it took forever to check in. Mom was her usual pleasant self, repeating her tirade from the county hospital: "I only wanted attention. I didn't really want to kill myself. I needed to go home and get my butt beat, and then I would be fine." The doctor who helped to check me in told her, "That may be true, but a suicide attempt is serious and she needs to be here." I was so glad when she finally left.

It was pretty late, so the nurse took me to my room and showed me the bathroom and everything I would need for the night. There was already someone sleeping in the room, so the nurse quietly told me that I would find out about schedules and such in the morning. I put my pajamas on and crawled into bed.

A few minutes later the nurse came back. She had a sleeping pill for me. I didn't really want to take it, but she said that with everything that had happened to me I wouldn't be able to sleep. After I took the pill, I thought I would never get to sleep. My mind wouldn't turn off. Worse yet, my roommate was crying softly, and I didn't know what to do. Next thing I knew, it was morning.

I wasn't sure what to expect. A male nurse came to wake me up and introduced me to my roommate, Julia. We went to breakfast, which the patients made themselves. I learned that everyone took turns at cooking for everyone else. I thought that was cool. After breakfast, we all cleaned the kitchen and then went to group.

I was introduced to everyone. It was really weird because I was the youngest one there. The next youngest person was twenty-four. The doctor explained that there was no place to put teenagers, but that I would be comfortable in a few days.

At group, everyone explained why they were in the hospital so I would know. There was a guy named Chuy. He had drunk bleach. I never knew anyone named Chuy. I felt sad that he'd drunk bleach to kill himself. He had a wife and kids and everything. At the end of group, the team—that's what the doctors call the patients—made the work plan for the next day. Every morning after group, the schedule was made for the next day. We had schedules for cooking, cleaning, crafts, and shopping duty. Everyone rotated through the positions. The schedule was made every day because people went home and new people came. I was going to help with shopping that afternoon after lunch.

After the morning group session, each patient went to see their own doctor to talk. I told my doctor that if I had to go home, I would just kill myself, and this time I would succeed.

He said, "We'll talk." I quickly learned that that was a standard answer for almost everything. Basically, during individual sessions, I just answered questions. Nothing was promised except that I would eventually go home. What a great promise!

On the first afternoon, we went grocery shopping. I was so surprised because we were not locked into the building or anything. Four of us went in a hospital van. We shopped at a normal grocery store and brought the food back for the next day. I thought it was cool to have so much freedom.

Every day pretty much followed the same schedule: breakfast, morning group, individual sessions, lunch, afternoon activities, afternoon group, dinner, individual time, movies, and bed. Even Saturday and Sunday were the same, except that there was a church service instead of morning group. But you didn't have to go—only if you wanted to. Saturday was family visit day.

After the first few days, everything became routine. I loved staying there. Andrea called me every day to see how I was. My mom never called. On the first Saturday, Mom and Dad came. I was really nervous when I heard they were both coming.

We sat in a room with my shrink. It was all so fake. Every accusation I had, they had an answer. My dad apologized and told me he had learned his lesson in jail. By this point in my life, I pretty much knew that the whole damn thing was his fault and that a few months in jail was nowhere near long enough for what he did to me. Mom and Dad spun their lies, and the doctor bought every word.

When they left, the doctor said, "Well, that went well, don't you think?"

I replied, "They are full of crap. Everything they said is a lie. Nothing will change when I go home. Can't you see that?"

"We'll see," he said.

I dreaded when I had to go home for a visit. I hated every second of it. Even David didn't understand. Of all people, I thought he would understand. The second time Mom and Dad came to family counseling, I just gave up, knowing the outcome was inevitable. I decided to enjoy the time I had there and learn all I could about coping with my emotions so that I could be strong. Little did I know that it would be harder to cope than I ever dreamed.

December 15
Dear Diary,

    Well, yesterday was interesting. My mom and dad were both there with the shrink. Both of them lied their heads off to him. I told them they were the reason I was in this place. They said things would change when I got home. I told the shrink they were lying and that nothing would change, it never did. I said I didn't want to go home. I said I wanted to go to a foster home. I said I would run away if they sent me back there. He said we would talk about it. I'm so not that stupid . . . that just means I am screwed . . .

December 23
Dear Diary,

    Oh yea, I'm home. Home sweet freaking home. At least it is only for a few days. David is coming tomorrow. That is good. Mom and dad took me to Burger King on the way home. Mom got mad because I pierced my ears. Man, she is so clueless. I did that three months ago, and now she notices! The shrink said I would have to see another shrink when I got home. Mom stated the expected: "Pull yourself up by your bootstraps." I wish someone would understand. Andrea understands. She isn't mad at me and hopes that the new shrink helps. I hope so too. I think my dad is sorry for what he did, but I also know that he will do it again the first time he gets a chance. What a pathetic slob! He says he is going to a psychiatrist and he has changed, but I see the way he looks at me.

December 25
Dear Diary,

David got me the most beautiful Bible. It is engraved. It says, "To my beloved sister." Isn't that the nicest thing you ever heard of? It is a Catholic Bible, but I don't care. I will never write in it, I will just keep it safe forever.

I love David more than anybody, but he doesn't really understand either. He said if I go back to the hospital, he will NEVER talk to me again. I have to go back . . . if I don't . . . I will be dead. I thought he might understand. I guess the people in my hospital group were right: I have to do what I have to do, even if the people I love don't agree. Of course Mom and Daphne don't want me to go back either. Everyone keeps saying how many problems I am causing. I don't care! I can't wait to go back. I wish I could stay there forever. At least it is safe. I don't have to worry about anyone hearing me cry. I can cry there, but I never cry at home.

December 25, part two.
Dear Diary,

Christmas is supposed to be about family, giving, Santa Claus, innocence . . . what a crock! I wish I could still believe in Santa Claus and innocence. That's kind of hard when one of my first memories is of my daddy giving me a bath, cleaning every nook and cranny, wherever those horrible fingers would reach.

I was so excited that I was going to see David, then I had to screw it all up by trying to kill myself! I am so glad I am in the hospital, but the only person in my family who loves me now hates me. I wish I would have just gone off by myself and done it - then I wouldn't feel anything. But I guess that wouldn't have worked. When I went to get Oskar out of class that morning, I didn't know what I was going to do. I just knew that I hurt so bad that I couldn't stand it anymore. I needed to be with someone who wanted nothing from me. I would have gone to Grace, but there is no way I could have asked her to ditch school.

Why did I do it? I don't really know what made me. All I know is that every day when I look in the mirror I see despair looking back. My eyes get darker every day—they are almost black instead of brown—and the pain keeps growing. No amount of drugs or sex makes the pain go away anymore. I can't even put a name to the pain; it just hurts so badly all the time. I can't sleep or eat or think. I can't even cry. I feel as if I am falling and falling and no one knows or cares. No one even notices. It just feels too hard to put on the mask anymore. I didn't even know what I was doing . . . I just wanted the anguish to go away and leave me alone.

I didn't even plan on trying to kill myself. The doctors are right. It is a cry for help. If someone would just acknowledge that my parents screwed me up, maybe it would help. If my parents would just admit—not lie—but really admit what they have done. That is just a delusion anyway, it will never happen.

So, here it is: the day when everyone is happy but me. I'm home with my family, and most importantly, my David. But all I want to do is go back to the hospital where it is safe. I wish someone got it. Why can't someone just understand? Why can't David understand?

December 28
Dear Diary,

   David asked me not to go back again yesterday, but I had to. I'm sorry he is mad at me, but I am so glad to be back. I even got my room back and still no roommate. Andrea called and told me she loves me and that I should just hang in there. She said the pictures from the dance came in and they are really nice. Matthias gave them to her for me. I'm glad she is my friend. Going back home for good will be so weird. I told my group that my mom doesn't want me to go see a shrink when I get home. They told me not to listen to her. I told my doctor I don't want to go home because my mom just thinks I am stupid and that I just want attention. Why can't she see that what my dad did to me messed me up? Good old doc thinks that after we talk again, she will understand. She won't, she will just pretend. Just like with everything. She says the right things when she has to, but then she stays the same. I bet she is enjoying her freedom screwing a different guy every night.

January 7
Dear Diary,

   Mom came to bring me home today. She brought the pictures from the dance. She was mad so I didn't stay home when I was grounded, but she didn't ground me again. Yea for her, what a great big step in the right direction! Maybe I should give her some brownie points.

The pictures are great. Well, they would be a lot better if it was Drew standing next to me, not Matthias. But anyway, I look nice and I'm still glad I went even if I did only get one dance with Drew.

I put the picture on my headboard so I can think about that night. I have to think about the good things because I really hate it here and don't want to be home.

Home from the Psych Ward

Things are so weird at home. Mom doesn't talk to me. Daphne tells me I'm stupid. David just looks at me like he doesn't know what to do with a crazy little sister. I don't think I'm crazy, but maybe I am. Who knows anymore anyway? I sure don't. God, why did I have to try to kill myself? I wish I would have succeeded. I wish all the time that I was back at the hospital.

Mom and Dad promised that they would change, but I doubt they will. I think Mom just wants to ignore the fact that Dad abused me. According to my group members, my mom abuses me too. I never really thought about it, but I guess leaving me home all the time, ignoring stuff about my dad, and smacking me across the face would be abuse. So all I can say to that is great. Now I have two abusive parents.

Dad feels like he paid his time in jail and things should just be peachy-keen between us. I don't think so. I guess I love him because he is my dad and all, but really, I think I hate him. How do you actually forgive something so bad in your life? I pray and ask how to forgive him. I ask people from church, but nothing seems to work. Sometimes, I think if I had a gun I'd kill him. I can't believe I feel guilty for him having sex with me. It was so not my fault. I don't know how I could have ever believed it was. I guess it's because you are supposed to be able to trust your parents.

They are supposed to love and protect from all harm. No one ever protected me. Sometimes I feel like the parent.

Going back to school will be really awful. Andrea said everyone in the whole school knows. I'll just play it cool, put on my mask, and hide my fears. If they had to go through what I went through, they would probably try to kill themselves too. I wish everyone would read To Kill a Mockingbird and listen to what Atticus tells Scout about seeing the other person's point of view.

At least I have some good friends who don't care how stupid I am. Andrea, Grace, and Oskar all tried to help. Too bad no one really knew how, but at least they were all there for me and tried to make my homecoming as easy as possible.

January 8
Dear Diary,

   Tina is so mad at me. She won't even talk to me. I guess after she found her grandma dead, I don't blame her. She has to live with the memory of going to her grandma's house after school and finding her grandma with her brains blown all over the room. I didn't think about anyone but myself. It was stupid to try to kill myself, but at least someone noticed that I needed help.

   Going back to school was weird, everyone knew and they all looked at me like I had a disease or something. Some people actually moved to the other side of the hall when they walked past me. I don't care - what do they know anyway?

   Drew talked to me. I thought he would be really freaked out, but he was nice about it. He told me it was okay and that he liked the cookies I baked him for Christmas. My heart beats so fast when he talks to me. I wonder if he knows what a fox he is and how much I like him.

   Sometimes I don't know how I can feel a normal emotion like having a crush on a boy when my life is such a mess. I have so many thoughts twirling in my head I feel like I just want to scream. There are so many conflicting emotions and I don't know what to do with all of them. So I write in hopes that it will help. It doesn't really, but I am good at pretending that things are fine.

January 11
Dear Diary,

Went to church tonight, had to get out of the house. I was high. Going to church high - what a life. Anyway, Jude drove me home and we talked about the hospital and everything. He told me it was okay and he understood. He said I had a right to feel the way I do and that my dad deserved to go to hell and I should be taken away from my mom. He said I could live with him, but he's not allowed. That was nice.

Every time he drives me home he kisses me. We have like this big affair or something. It's really weird because I haven't told anyone at all, and we are just all normal at church. As soon as he drops the other girls off, we pull over and park for like an hour. We never make out in front of my house. It's like all secret and everything. He is a good kisser. He has felt up my shirt, but nowhere else. It's strange because he is a grown-up and it seems like he goes way slow. Most guys only think about getting inside my pants. The first time he touched my breasts, I was really nervous because they are so small. But he said he liked how they felt. He told me thank you for letting him touch me. Weird. So it is this routine now: we park, kiss, he feels me up, then takes me home. He never said he loves me and I'm glad. It would be too weird if he loved me. I think he is just horny because Liliana won't give him any until after they are married. We talked about it a couple of times. He wonders if he will get anything after they get married.

January 15
Dear Diary,

Mom finally made my appointment and I went to see my shrink today. I got to leave school for most of the day because I had to ride my bike. It is pretty far, but I love to ride my bike and just be by myself. It has been weird to be in school all day long anyway. I really needed the break.

Her name is Anne. She seems nice. When I told her I was getting high, she didn't even care. She said that I needed medicine and then I wouldn't feel like getting high all the time. Mom was so pissed when I gave her the prescription. She said she wasn't going to get it for me because there was nothing that a swift kick in my rear wouldn't cure. I told her I would call Anne and they would take me away again. Witch!

Anne, the Shrink

I see Anne once a week. I get out of school, and I ride my bike because Mom says, "I have to sleep after working all the time. You made this mess. You can damn well get yourself there if it's so important to you. I won't take you." She went once and was so mad after Anne talked to her. I don't really know what happened when they talked, but I guess Anne told Mom that I wasn't faking and she better believe me.

I like to go to my sessions. They don't last long enough though. Sometimes we are right in the middle of a big conversation and the damn buzzer rings. No matter what we are talking about, the buzzer is god and I have to leave. We talk about all kinds of things: family, school, friends, drugs. I know Anne doesn't like me doing drugs, but she doesn't hassle me about it either. She still says that once the medicine takes effect, I won't need drugs anymore. I don't really think the medicine does anything but make me sleepy.

The thing I hate about my appointments is that Mom is always pissed at me. Life sucks enough without her having another reason to hate me. Every time I go, Mom gives me dirty looks all day long. One time, I asked her what her problem was, and she said; "You are the one with the problem. I never had to go to a shrink. Pull yourself up by your bootstraps and grow up." I wish I had some bootstraps to pull myself up with.

Anne tells me not to worry about what my mom says, but it's really hard. She's not the one living there and getting crap every day.

Since I got back from the hospital and have been seeing Anne, at least I go to school. I haven't cut class once. So that's one less thing for Mom to gripe about.

January 16
Dear Diary,

   Mom brought home my medicine this morning. I saw it in my bathroom. Of course, she didn't say anything to me about it. She would rather just ignore me and everything that has to do with the reality of my dad abusing me. I got a letter from David today. He said he was sorry he gave me a hard time and that he hoped I was okay. He said he hates the Air Force. I feel sorry for him. Mom made him go even though he didn't want to. She just wanted him out of her hair. I bet if I ran away forever she would be so happy.

January 18
Dear Diary,

   Drew came by today, he just came by. Can you believe it? He said he was out running, getting ready for a cross-country meet and he just wanted to stop by. Wow. We sat on the front porch and talked for a long time. I wanted him to kiss me so bad, but it was enough that he stopped by. I need to learn to be happy with what I get. That is what Anne told me. I like her.

January 29
Dear Diary,

   This has been the best two weeks. Drew formally asked me to be his girlfriend. He gave me his class ring. He is the best kisser in the world. I still can't believe that he would want to go out with someone like me. We have been together every day. I haven't even wanted a joint this week. I wonder if it is Drew or the medicine Anne gave me. Anyway, he is a virgin. That is funny because he is so damn foxy that who would imagine he is a virgin? He took me to the movies and out to dinner and everything. He is like a real boyfriend. He doesn't say "Wham, bam, thank you ma'am" and leave. He doesn't even want to have sex. That is weird, but kind of nice.

I saw Timothy at school today, and he looked at me kind of strange. I wonder why? I wonder if he still has feelings for me. I think his parents made him break up with me, so maybe he does and now that he doesn't have a girlfriend anymore, and he sees me with Drew, maybe that is weird for him. But I don't care, because I love Drew.

The whole Jude thing is weird too. I told him I couldn't kiss him anymore because I have a boyfriend now. He said he kissed me with a fiancé, and why couldn't I kiss him? I told him it would just be weird. He looked all hurt and stuff. What a mess I got myself into. I asked him if he would still give me rides home. He said he would, but he was all sad and pouting. I really don't need a guilt trip from Jude right now; things are too good for me to feel bad about not kissing someone who is not my boyfriend.

Drew, Mr. All-American

Drew is one of the cutest guys I have ever laid eyes on. He has these incredible blue eyes and this mouth with these full lips. Oh, man! I have had a crush on him ever since I first saw him at the beginning of the year. The thing is, it is not really a crush anymore. Over the months I have known him, we had some good conversations, and I really like him for who he is. He gets good grades, is in sports, works at a restaurant, and plays in the school jazz band.

I didn't think I would ever have a chance with someone like him, but it turned out I was wrong. Maybe all of my flirting paid off. Right before Christmas, I made cookies for everyone. When I gave Drew his cookies, I said; "What I really want to give you for Christmas is a kiss, but since I'm not your girlfriend, I can't." He just kind of laughed and patted me on the head. I felt like such an idiot. Well, not an idiot exactly, more like a little kid.

I was pretty surprised when he actually came to my house and wanted to go out with me. I think that dating Drew will be good for me. I don't want to mess this up, so I am not being stupid and doing drugs because he is against that. I feel so good about myself because I am going out with one of the most popular seniors in the school. His friends are pretty nice, and they all accept me even though they know I'm a stoner. Eddy and Amy are the best. It's like they have accepted me as their little sister and try to give me advice and stuff. I like how Drew makes me feel. If it is possible for me to love someone, I love Drew.

February 2
Dear Diary,

Last night was wonderful. Mom was at her art class. I said I didn't feel good, so I didn't go. Drew came over. We were in my room making out and I asked him if he wanted to lose his virginity. He said yes. So we fooled around some more and then we made love. Not sex, love. I liked initiating Drew into sex. He is such a good kisser and I really wanted to have sex with him to show him that I love him. It was so great making love to him. After it was over, he asked me if I was okay. He said it was really nice and he was glad I was his first. He asked me if we could do it again. Isn't that cute? We were lying together in my bed, almost asleep when I heard my mom. The stupid witch came home early. Drew rolled off the bed by the wall. He was parked across the street; she probably doesn't even know what kind of car he drives anyway. She didn't come in my room, but even if she did, she wouldn't have seen him. She left for work about 20 minutes later. Drew was really scared; I told him it was okay, not to worry about it. He thought I would get in trouble. That is so sweet. He stayed with me until 1 am. We just kissed and talked all that time. It was great. I wish we could spend every night like that.

I had an appointment with Anne today and told her about Drew. She said he sounds great. She gave me the name of a clinic so I could get some birth control. I will go next week. Andrea's mom will take me. I told her mom was still giving me crap about the medicine. She asked me if I felt better. I said yes, so she said don't worry about what my mom says. I think she sees right through my mom. For one thing, my mom refuses to come to another appointment with me. That pisses Anne off. I don't think she likes my mom very much. I'm glad. This is the first time I feel like a grownup understands that my mom really is a liar; it isn't just kid talk.

February 14
Dear Diary,

Valentine's Day. Guess what? Drew got me the best present. It is a gold chain. I could not believe it. It is so pretty, he spent so much money on it. I told him that it was too much and he shouldn't have done that. He just told me to turn around. He put in on my neck, turned me back around and told me it was beautiful just like me. He said he wanted to show me how much he loved me. Man, he is just so nice. I don't know what he sees in me, but I'm glad he loves me because I would die without him.

We went bowling, then parking. He brought a bottle of wine. We drank some then started making out. He moved the car to the back of the parking lot. We made love again. We have been doing it whenever we can now that I am on the pill and we don't have to worry about getting pregnant. He really likes having sex with me and after every time he thanks me for letting him. He is so sweet!

Grace is mad that I am having sex with him, but it isn't sex anyway. This is the first time that it has been love and I want to show him all the time how much I love him. I know she thinks it is wrong because of God and everything, but she just doesn't understand. At least she is still my friend anyway. I would make love to him a million times just to hear him thank me for letting him. This is the first time I really wanted to have sex and I really care for the person. Before, sex was just something to do and I didn't care one way or the other. Now it means something. I actually don't even like the sex part that much, but I love how it makes Drew feel. He is so happy. It makes me glad to make him happy.

February 20
Dear Diary,

    David came home today. He got kicked out of the Air Force because of drugs in his locker. He said they weren't his, but I don't care. I am just glad he is home. Mom is being so mean to him though. All she does is call him a lazy worthless piece of crap. How can she say that to her own son? He never wanted to go to the stupid Air Force anyway! I bet she wouldn't care if we all died.

February 28
Dear Diary,

    The one thing I really like about school is choir. Mr. Meddows is great. He never was weird to me after the suicide thing and he likes that his favorite student, Drew, and I are together. I love to sing. It expresses me just like writing poems. There is going to be a musical. I want to try out. It will be so fun. Drew will be in the band, playing his trumpet. I wonder if that is why he kisses so good, all that puckering.

Choir

Choir is the best class ever invented. I love to sing. Genevieve and Andrea are in my class and that makes it fun. There are only a few freshmen in the class. It was really intimidating at the beginning of the year, but now it's just normal. I sing soprano and Genevieve and Andrea sing alto. We sing pretty good songs, and it is just a fun class to be in. It is the one really relaxing thing about my day.

When we had a Christmas concert, Grace came to see me sing, but my mom didn't. I don't think she has ever been to a school event—never ever. It used to bug me a lot, but now I just blow it off. It would be nice if she showed up to things once in a while, but she never has. I guess I am kind of used to it.

My favorite song from choir is "Bridge Over Troubled Water." I don't know why I like that one so much. I just do. I like to sing in church too. They should let kids in the church choir. I don't think they would let me in anyway. Most of the adults look at me like I am the spawn of the devil or something. I can't help it if my parents are divorced and don't go to church. People are so dumb! I like when we sing at youth group. I think I sing good, but I'm not really sure. It doesn't matter anyway. It makes me happy.

PART 4

Spring

March 3
Dear Diary,

Musical tryouts were today. I have been really sick, and I couldn't sing well at all because of my throat. I just got over having mononucleosis for a month. I didn't make the cut. That really bites! I really wanted to be in the play. Andrea got a part, Drew will be playing in the pit, and Eddy will play the main character. The play is Joseph and the Amazing Technicolor Dreamcoat. It is going to be really good. Even though I won't be singing, I will still help anyway; I can paint scenes.

March 7
Dear Diary,

Daphne was making dinner. She was using a butcher knife to pry apart frozen hamburgers. The knife slipped and it almost cut her finger off. I yelled for Mom to come to the kitchen. When she got there, Daphne was staring at her hand, blood dripping all over the meat, the counter and floor. She was laughing uncontrollably. Mom said that she was in hysterics. I knew that she was high as a kite and that is what made it funny to her. Mom had me get a towel and wrap Daphne's finger, then she told me to clean up the mess while she took Daphne to the hospital. As they were leaving, she was yelling at Daphne for always being so accident prone. "I've had to spend more time dragging your butt to the hospital, blah, blah, blah . . ."

At least Daphne probably won't remember how mean Mom was being because she is so wasted. I hope she is okay, but it was pretty stupid of her to try to pry apart frozen hamburgers with a butcher knife!

March 15
Dear Diary,

Daphne's b-day, a huge party. What a big surprise. As soon as Mom left for work, here come all the stoners. School tomorrow and 200 idiots in my house. Everyone was so wasted. I didn't even have to smoke any pot to get high. There were so many drugs in the house; coke, smack, LSD, PCP, shrooms, the list goes on . . . Stefan's gross brother, Damien, cornered me in the bathroom and told me if he sucked my boobs they would grow. Man, what a gross pig. Like I would really let that pig touch me. He stinks and doesn't even brush his teeth. Besides the fact that he's like 26. What a loser. Stupid Daphne passed out around 4 and I had to kick everyone out. I dragged her to bed and cleaned up the house, then had to go to school. Oh well. I'm used to going to school with no sleep.

March 17
Dear Diary,

David and Mom got in a big fight and David left last night. He took everything. No one knows where he is. Mom doesn't even care. She said she was glad that the "lazy son of a . . ." was gone. How can you say that about your own kid? She is seriously screwed up. I hate her so much. I hate this family. Why did David have to leave without me? Why couldn't he take me with him? Where are you David? I don't want to be left here all alone.

March 18
Dear Diary,

Mom's birthday today. I tried to make it really special for her, but all she did was grouch around the house. I bought her some art supplies from my babysitting money. It cost a lot. She didn't even say thank you. She went out without telling me where she was going. She didn't come home.

March 19
Dear Diary,

Drew has been working too much. I hardly ever get to see him anymore. I think he might break up with me. I hope not. I will die. He is the one thing that has kept me going the past few months. How can I go on without him? If he breaks up with me it will just prove what a loser I am. I shouldn't worry about it. I am just being paranoid, I hope.

March 20
Dear Diary,

Drew broke up with me. He is seeing Delilah—freaking beautiful, perfect cheerleader, track star, A student! How could he do this to me? We never even had a fight. How could she steal the only happy thing I have ever had in my life? She has a perfect life. She didn't need him. I need him. Oh God, my stomach hurts. My whole self hurts. I just want to die.

March 21
Dear Diary,

    When Jude was driving me home tonight he asked what was wrong. I told him Drew broke up with me. He said he was so sorry and that I deserved better. He said if he didn't have to be engaged to Liliana, he would love to be my boyfriend. He was driving someone's van, I don't know whose. We parked and went and sat in the back to talk. The next thing I knew, he was kissing me. One thing led to another and pretty soon we screwed. I didn't even care. I didn't feel anything. I just went away somewhere else like when my dad was raping me. Nothing matters anymore.

    Now I just feel stupid and dirty. I didn't even want to have sex with him; it just happened. I miss Drew. I wish I was dead.

Heartbreak, Again

When Drew broke up with me, I just wanted to die. It's harder than anything because I actually trusted him and gave him my heart. I trusted Drew with everything.

I feel just like I did before I went to the hospital. I think about killing myself all the time. The only reason I don't is that Grace asked me not to. I know she loves me, and I don't want to hurt her. I will keep my promise to Grace even if it kills me to do it.

I hurt all the time. My eyes grow blacker and blacker every day. I never sleep. I just listen to the radio and cry. I write sad poems and then rip them up because I will never give them to Drew anyway. I knew it would never last. How could he love someone like me anyway? But knowing doesn't make it any easier. I know I am crap already, and his breaking up with me just reinforces everything.

Oskar and I went to the creek to talk. We talked about Anne. He said, "How's it all going with her anyway?" I said, "The medicine doesn't help and every time I need a refill, my mom gets so pissed at me." I was so frustrated that I just took the bottle out of my purse and threw it in the middle of the creek. Oskar was so worried. He said, "Why the hell did you do that?" I said, "I just don't want the hassle anymore. It isn't worth all of the fighting. Besides, drugs make me feel way better than any stupid medicine."

The next time I went to see Anne, I told her that I wasn't coming back anymore. She was upset and asked why. I said, "I don't need you anymore. Things are great." I knew she didn't believe me and I felt like a jerk for lying to her. I just don't need the hassle. Things suck enough without adding to the problem. I made it this far by myself. I guess I can do it some more.

March 23

Dear Diary,

Genevieve is really sick of her parents. They only pay attention to Coline and her little brother. I don't think her parents are as bad as she thinks, but I know what it feels like to be ignored all the time. We are making some great plans. Freedom!

March 25

Dear Diary,

I am moving! At least that's what I told Mr. Meddows and everyone else. Friday is the day.

March 27

Dear Diary,

Well, we did it. Genevieve and I packed and hid our stuff in my garage. We went to my bank today and took out all my money. It was only $150, but it should get us by for a while. We took the bus to Vasona Park and here we are. We will spend the night and go to Santa Cruz tomorrow. Genevieve seems scared. It is the first time she ever ran away. We bought some Ding-Dongs and Coke for dinner. It was kind of scary going into a store. We waited until school was out so no one would get suspicious and call the cops. We are hiding in a little cave of bushes so no one will see us. We will sleep here tonight. I am just trying to make sure Genevieve doesn't get too scared.

March 30
Dear Diary,

   Well, we made it to Santa Cruz after hitching a ride from the park. We waited all day for Genevieve's friend to get home from work. He was sure surprised to see us, but didn't have a problem letting us crash there until we could figure out what we wanted to do and where to go. I wish I knew where David was, I would go find him and live with him.

Running Away

I have run away a lot in the past few years, but I always went home when Mom threatened me. I have never gone this far though. I usually just went to a friend's house. This time, there is nothing to go home for. David is gone and no cares but me. Drew doesn't care about me, and Grace will get over me. She will actually be better off without having me to worry about.

I'm glad I ended up in Santa Cruz. It's one of my favorite places. The ocean is where I feel peaceful. It is calm and beautiful. I would like to stay here forever but can't sponge off Genevieve's friend. That would just be wrong. I would like just to get a job, but I look way younger than my fourteen years. I went to a couple of businesses today, and they all told me to go home. I was too young to be working.

I think I will just be a whore. It can't be any worse than what my dad did to me. At least I can make some money and not have to worry about anyone but myself. I just can't think of any other way to make money. I wonder how you start being a whore. I'll think about it more tomorrow.

April 1
Dear Diary,

April Fools. I ran away with a fool, no, that's mean. She can't help if she is just a scared little kid. Genevieve called her parents last night. My mom called this morning and said the cops were on their way to get me if I wasn't home by noon. Genevieve's friend drove us home, lecturing us all the way about how much better off we would be with our parents. Home sweet home again.

April 5
Dear Diary,

Well, another great day in the wonderful life of me. Mom made me quit helping on the musical. I am grounded for the rest of my life. Drew won't even say hi. Genevieve is not allowed to talk to me, not even at school. Everything sucks. I miss David. I wish I knew where he was. Mom and Daphne don't even give a damn about me or that David is gone. What is wrong with them anyway? Maybe it's just me that's wrong. Maybe I really am crazy.

April 6
Dear Diary,

Daphne and Mom got in a huge fight today. I don't even know what started it. I was in my room listening to my Boston record. All of a sudden, I heard all of this yelling and then two slaps. Daphne went to her room and slammed the door, then I heard Mom on the phone. I went into the kitchen and asked her what was going on. She told me to mind my own business and get back in my room.

    A while later, the doorbell rang and I heard mom talking to the cops. I opened my door a crack so I could hear her. She told them that Daphne hit her and she wanted her out of the house. Mom told Daphne to get her butt out of her room. I heard Daphne tell the cops the only reason she slapped my mom was because my mom slapped her first, and she was sick of getting hit. The cops asked Mom what she wanted to do. My mom said, "Lock her up and throw away the key."

    So the cops took Daphne away to juvie. When they left, I went out of my room and yelled at my mom for sending Daphne to juvie. I couldn't believe she did that. She yelled at me, "Shut up. You better watch yourself or the same thing will happen to you." I ran out of the house, slamming the door behind me as hard as I could.

    I walked to JS Elementary School and sat on the swings and cried. I don't even know how long I was there, except that it was totally dark and really late when I got home. Mom had locked the front door, but my window was open so I just went in that way. I can't believe she sent Daphne to juvie. Doesn't she know what happens there? Doesn't she care at all? She is so screwed up! I hope Daphne will be okay there.

April 8
Dear Diary,

    I stole 100 bucks from Mom today. I don't even feel bad because she never buys me anything. I work for all my own stuff or steal it if I can't afford it. Stefan hooked me up with a guy in Sunnyvale. We got some great coke and Sinsemilla for the money. Stefan, Oskar, and I went to JS Elementary School and got so wasted. Coke and weed together is really a strange feeling, both up and down at the same time. I even have some reserves left. I gave the coke to the guys. I will save the weed for when I need to just get away from it all.

April 9
Dear Diary,

   Daphne came home from juvie today. She said she's never talking to Mom again. She is packing everything she owns.

April 10
Dear Diary,

   Daphne moved out today when Mom was gone. She told me she would come get me when she got settled and I could live with her. I asked her where she was going but she told me not to worry about it. She would be fine and she didn't want Mom to know where she was. When Mom got home she yelled for Daphne to get her butt out of her room. I just stayed in my room. I heard her going down the hall, telling Daphne how much trouble she was going to be in for not coming when called. I heard Daphne's door open, then Mom opened my door and started yelling at me, asking where Daphne went. I told her I didn't know and it served her right for sending Daphne to juvie. She started yelling at me that she was glad

Daphne was gone and if Daphne thought she could come crawling home she was sadly mistaken, blah, blah, blah... I just tuned her out as best as I could. After she left, I cried because she is so mean to her kids. First David, now Daphne.

I am truly all alone now.

April 12
Dear Diary,

Oskar and I went to JS Elementary School yesterday. He had a fifth of Jack Daniels and I took a bottle of coke from home. We just sat around talking about everything and drinking. We must have been there for hours. Pretty soon the bottle was gone. I don't even know how I got home. Oskar called Jaimey and Ruth to come and help me. Jaimey used to rent a room from us, and his wife Ruth is a stewardess. Oskar knew he was pretty cool. Oskar must have been pretty scared to call an adult for help, but that was actually a good choice of who to call. All I remember is I was in bed and Jaimey and Ruth were there. I totally blacked out. I don't have any idea what happened. I didn't get in trouble. What can she do, ground me for two lives? She doesn't care enough to do anything anyway. Jaimey called today to see if I was okay. I asked if I did anything stupid. He said, "Oh, other than drinking a fifth of JD?" Okay, good point. I guess it was stupid. He told me to be careful and not to do stupid stuff anymore.

I have been scaring myself lately. There have been too many times when I don't remember what happened. I don't know where I was, who I was with, how I got home, what happened, nothing. I need to clean up. The blackouts are scaring me.

Drinking and Drugs

In the past three years, I have done so many different drugs. The only thing I have not tried is heroin, and I don't think I will. No one around here does that crap anyway. I have been drinking steadily since seventh grade. I guess I am an alcoholic, but I don't care. Well, I guess sometimes I do, but mostly I don't.

My dad gave me beer to drink out of his can ever since I can remember. He thought it was cute. He said, "Fred, come and have a drink with your daddy." I don't know why he called me Fred. Maybe he wanted a boy. I would have been better off if I was a boy. Then, with Daphne and all her partying and friends giving me drugs, I guess my habits were inevitable.

Lately though, I have been doing more and more drugs, and I don't get high fast enough. I guess I have built up a resistance. I need more and more to feel anything, or actually to feel numb. I hardly eat or sleep. I just do drugs. I don't go to class much. What is the use? I only see Drew and his gorgeous, not-screwed-up girlfriend, Delilah, everywhere I turn. Living just hurts too much.

I am starting to scare myself with all the drugs. When I look in the mirror, I don't know who is looking back. My eyes are so scary—empty of all emotion. Maybe I have sold my soul.

April 15
Dear Diary,

   Oskar is so awesome. I'm so glad we're friends. He told me he was sorry for letting me get so messed up. He didn't know that I would black out.

   So now, instead of doing so many drugs, I just sit at Stefan's and get high, and then we screw. He's okay in bed. At least he doesn't pretend it's something it isn't. We both know we are just using each other. Actually, I don't even know why I have sex with him. I guess because as soon as we start, off go the emotions. It is a good way to hide. At least Stefan won't screw and tell. According to half of BHS, I have screwed the other half. It would be nice if I deserved the reputation I have. Oh well, who the hell cares anyway?

   Things are still weird with Jude, no they are weirder now. Now he feels all guilty and told me he shouldn't have cheated on Liliana and he's sorry for screwing me. Whatever man!

   I wonder what Oskar thinks of the men in my life. I think he thinks I am stupid and I really don't want him to think that. He is too much of a friend to have him think bad crap about me. But if he is such a good friend, why can't I share what I really feel? Will there ever be anyone I can totally open up to? Will I always hide behind this mask?

April 18
Dear Diary,

   Grace told me about church summer camp today. I want to go, but I know my stupid mom won't pay for it or let me go. It would be cool to go though. I could go away for a whole week. The camp, Hume Lake, is in the mountains. It would be so great to be in the mountains again. I really hate the city. When I am grown up, I will live in the mountains or by the beach.

April 21
Dear Diary,

   Guess what? During youth group tonight, Jude told me that I was going to camp. I asked him how and he said that there was a scholarship for me. I called my mom from the church and she said yes. Anything to get rid of me for a week, but I don't care—I will be rid of her too. Maybe I will have a chance with Timothy again. Probably not. I don't even know why I bother to dream. It is his last year for camp.

April 26
Dear Diary,

   School is almost over. Every time I see Drew and Delilah together it hurts so much. I can't believe that I can feel so much pain. I thought I was dead to pain. Not dead enough, obviously. Even the drugs and sex don't dull the hurt and emptiness inside. Delilah will be at prom by his side. It was supposed to be me. I wonder if they have sex. It hurts so bad that he is sharing his love with her. I am the one that showed him. I am the one that gave myself to him. Oh man, why can't he just look at me and see that I love him? She just loves the attention of being Mr. All-American-Boy's girl.

April 27
Dear Diary,

Daphne came by today to see me when Mom wasn't home. She said she was doing fine. She had a job and an apartment with some people. She asked me not to tell Mom. Yeah, like I would tell her anything anyway. She has never even mentioned David or Daphne's names. I think she hates us all. I just try to keep the house clean and stay in my room when she is home.

April 31
Dear Diary,

Prom is tonight. This sucks so bad. I should be there, dancing with Drew. I should be in his arms, kissing his lips, loving his body. But I'm not. Why? Because I am nothing but a dirty little whore! I should have known that it couldn't last - how could he love someone like me? There is nothing good in me. I don't know why I even bother to live. Maybe I should just kill myself. Who would care anyway? Dad? Mom? Daphne? David would if he knew, I think. I guess Grace would care. Living just hurts so bad all the time. Why can't I just be normal? Why do I have this turmoil all the time? I am tired, so very tired of everything. Why did God even let me be born? Why doesn't he just let me die?

May 3
Dear Diary,

   Drew and Delilah broke up. It doesn't matter because he still doesn't want me. I hope she feels as much pain as I did, but she doesn't. She didn't love him. Stupid idiot - takes him away and doesn't even care. I see her walking and laughing in the halls with her friends, like she doesn't have a care in the world.

   Today Mr. Meddows told his aides he would take us on his boat Saturday. I will go just so I don't have to be home.

May 5
Dear Diary,

   Sailing is fun. I never knew. Mr. Meddows's wife is really nice. Only Tad and I showed up, so there was lots of food to eat. Mr. Meddows keeps his boat at the marina in Santa Cruz. We sailed all day. We got to dive off the boat and swim. That was really neat. Mrs. Meddows made us hot dogs on a grill, but she put them inside a tortilla with cheese and salsa instead of in a bun with mustard and ketchup. I never tasted anything so good. That was really nice of Mr. Meddows to take us, especially me. I asked him why he took me after I lied to him about moving. He said that everyone makes mistakes and I was a good person anyway. That was cool. Most adults just think I'm a total screwup. I don't care anyway. Well, maybe I do. It's just so much easier not to care.

May 10
Dear Diary,

My freshman year is almost over. I don't know what I will do this summer. Mom wants me to go stay with Dad. What the hell is wrong with her anyway? I'm not going. I will run away again and never come home! Stupid witch. Doesn't she ever think of anyone but herself? Well, that was a stupid question. Of course she doesn't. Hasn't she proven that time after time?

May 15
Dear Diary,

I saw Timothy at school today. He looked at me weird. Kinda like he wanted to say something to me. I didn't really know what to do, so I walked away. I just don't want to get hurt again. But now I keep thinking about the way he looked at me and wondering what he wanted to say. Was it just my imagination? He really looked like he misses me, but why would he? I can't talk to anyone about this, so I just write. I think Grace might be glad if we got back together. She wouldn't have to worry about the whole sex thing because Timothy is a nice boy. Oh yea, nice boy + bad girl = will never happen. How could I be so stupid to even think about it?

Speaking of Grace, I don't know how I would have made it through this year without her family. Her parents let me eat and sleep there all the time. They even listen when I have a question during their Bible study. I believe in God, but it's so hard. How could the God they talk about let the stuff go on in the world that happens? Why do innocent children have to suffer? I just don't get it all. It makes my head hurt.

May 20
Dear Diary,

I went to graduation today. Goodbye to Eddy, Amy, Drew, and Timothy. I will always remember all of you. Each of you has impacted my life. Even through the heartache, I am glad to have known you.

May 22
Dear Diary,

Mom wouldn't buy me a yearbook and I couldn't afford one, but at least I got the autograph papers. Alex wrote, "I was the first one in your crack" in my autograph section. What an idiot!

May 23
Dear Diary,

Boy, I guess I have made a great impression on people this year. I looked over all of my autographs when I was by myself. Almost everyone wrote stuff about partying and sex, getting stoned and not getting caught, and how much fun I was to be around at the parties. What a waste of a year. Man, I am such a loser. My whole life is one big happy party, moving from one drug to the next and one guy to the next.

If only people could see what was on the inside — if only they really knew. My life is not a happy party. People are just too self-centered to see beyond their own lives. They have no idea of what is really behind the mask I wear for the world. I don't even know if I know what is behind the mask—who I really am inside. Sometimes I think that I am nothing but a loser. But then I think about people like Timothy, Eddy, Amy, Drew, Grace. They all say there is more to me than the drugs and alcohol. They all say there is a good person underneath all of the crap. Are they right? Is there someone good in there?

May 27
Dear Diary,

Today is the last day of my freshman year. What do I have to show for it? I'm a little taller, not much though. I have slept with people I do not give a damn about. I have been in love two times, but in totally different ways.

I passed two classes: choir and aiding. I have scars on my body that will heal, but scars inside that no one sees or cares about. I ran away. I rode in a cop car. I went to the psych ward. I ran away again. I maintained a bad reputation. I lost some awesome friends: Genevieve, Tina, and Timothy. I made some friends: Eddy, Amy, and maybe Drew?

All in all, it is another screwed-up year in the wonderful life of me.

PART 5

Summer

June 5
Dear Diary,

   Daphne called the house today to ask Mom if I could come spend a week with her. Mom didn't even ask her how she was or where she was living. She just said, "Yeah, come get her."

June 6
Dear Diary,

   Daphne came and got me today. She lives with a whole bunch of people. She said everyone just kind of crashes there and everyone helps pay for the rent and food. The apartment is full of stoners, and everyone just crashes on the floor or wherever they pass out. There isn't a time when someone is not lighting up a joint or snorting some coke.

June 8
Dear Diary,

   We went to the park down the block today to buy some drugs. Daphne and her friends were just trading the money for the pot when a cop car pulled into the park. Everyone ran. It was really scary. I didn't know where I was so I couldn't get home if Daphne and her friends got caught. We hid behind a 7-Eleven in an alley. We saw the cops catch the guy that was selling the pot to Daphne and her friends. When they drove away, we walked home. Daphne and her friends were laughing about it and saying how they would need to find a new supplier. I didn't think it was very funny. I was really scared. Daphne has a record because of Mom and if she gets caught she will go to real jail. I told her she better clean up, but she just told me not to worry, she could take care of herself.

June 10
Dear Diary,

Even though I have been trying so hard to stay away from getting so wasted, it is really hard staying with Daphne. You get high from just being in the room. All of her friends think I am funny. I don't really like them. None of them except for Daphne has a real job. They all just sell drugs and get high. There is always someone different here. Some of the people are kind of scary. Damien comes by a lot and he always looks at me like he's undressing me with his eyes. He is such a creep! I asked Daphne why she lets him in her house. She said there is nothing wrong with him other than the fact that he doesn't shower. I don't believe her. I think he is evil. He scares me.

June 12
Dear Diary,

I spent the entire week wasted out of my brain, just because you can't get away from the drugs in Daphne's house. I'm glad she is out of Mom's house and she seems to be happy. I don't think I would want to live there though. There are too many people in and out all the time. Once, someone got some bad acid and he totally wigged out. Some of the guys just picked him up, took him outside, and dumped him there. I thought that was mean. Everyone kept offering me all kinds of stuff. It was like I was a little kid and they were trying to give me candy or something. "Here, Kim, try this one. It is really good. You will like it." I did not try the heroin and after that guy wigged out, I wouldn't drop any acid. They all made fun of me, but I don't care. I know what can happen if you get some bad stuff. I don't want to be dumped outside all by myself. It's just like the drug scenes in Go Ask Alice. I'm glad not to be home, but this isn't much better.

June 15
Dear Diary,

    Daphne was really mad when I told her I was ready to go home. I didn't want to make her mad, but I had to get ready for camp. At least that was the reason I gave her. She asked me why I even wanted to go. She said I could just stay there for the summer and not go to stupid camp. I told her I couldn't because someone paid for me to go to camp and it would be mean to waste that money. She thought I would just be glad to get away from Mom. I was, but I didn't like all those strangers. I didn't feel safe. Besides, I want to go to camp. I get to go to the mountains and be with people that are nice for a whole week. Everyone complains about going to chapel all the time, but I like it. I like the songs and I like listening to the speakers.

I like playing the games and going to the cove to go swimming. I like hanging out with my friends without having to sneak out of the house to do something with people from church.

June 20
Dear Diary,

I have been cleaning the house since I got home from Daphne's. Mom told me it had to be perfect or she wouldn't let me go. Tomorrow I am going to summer camp. I am glad to go to get away from home and to hang out with Grace, Caitlin, and Gwen.

June 21
Dear Diary,

I don't know what the deal is, but something about camp this year is different. I feel different. I have tried so hard to be a Christian since I first went to church, but it has been so hard because of everything I have been through. I don't know how to be a Christian and every time I try, I fail. I am the world's biggest backslider - in other words - LOSER! Anyway, this time I feel totally different inside. Things that the speakers are saying are really hitting home. Can I really change? Is it possible?

June 22
Dear Diary,

Tonight, after service, I waited to talk to the speaker, Reese. I had to wait like an hour to be alone with him. I asked if he minded if I talked to him and that it might take a while. He said he didn't mind. Well, I told him about my dad and asked if God was really so concerned about me, how could he let my dad rape me time after time? I prayed as a child. I was innocent. I didn't ask for it. Nothing ever helped. The abuse just continued and it got worse as I got older. I can't understand how God could allow a little child to be hurt like that.

Reese said he wanted to ask me a question. He said, "Why not you? Out of all the people in the world, what makes you so special over everyone else? Aren't there others in pain? Why not you?"

At first, I didn't really understand. I asked him if God made this happen to me.

Reese told me that the Bible says it rains on the just and unjust. Bad things happen to good people; good things happen to bad people. That is just the way the world is because of sin. What matters is what we do with our lives. Although no one should have to go through what I went through, it happens because of the world we live in, because people choose sin, not because God makes it happen. Now I have a choice, I can allow God to use me to help other girls in my situation or I can continue to live in pain - avoiding the past.

Wow, I am totally blown away. No one ever explained God that way before. So if God didn't allow this to happen and bad things happen to good people, it is up to me to decide what to do with it. I know I won't have a pity party for myself. I have never been that way - it's just so hard to figure everything out. I have cried more tonight than I have in years. I have so much to think about, but I'm so tired. I think I'll go to bed now and think about this more tomorrow.

June 23
Dear Diary,

Reese called me over after the morning service and asked if I minded if he shared my story with one of the counselors. I said I guess not, if he thought he should. After lunch one of the counselors, Monica, said she wanted to talk to me. She told me that Reese had told her about me and she just wanted to know if I wanted to talk and get a woman's perspective.

I talked to her about everything I had been thinking about last night. How could I help people? Why would anyone want to listen to me? How could I really change? I have tried and tried and always failed. Monica said that it is okay to fall down as long as I get up and try again. We talked for such a long time. I told her about the meaningless sex and drugs. I told her about Timothy and how I loved him so much but knew he was better off without me. I told her about the suicide attempts and how most of the time I just didn't care anymore. I told her that this time things felt so different, but that I am scared because things have been different before and I always fall back into my old habits. I was scared that this was just a "mountaintop experience" and it would all go away as soon as I got home.

Monica told me now is the time for decisions. The first thing I need to do is to make some goals for myself. So, after we talked, I went back to my room and wrote what I wanted to do differently and what would make me fall back into bad patterns. It breaks down to this: I want to stop drugs because then everything else will be easier. I can't make good decisions if I am wasted on drugs or alcohol. I can't stop the drugs in the neighborhood because it would be too hard. I can't do it by myself. But how to solve this dilemma?

June 25
Dear Diary,

I called Mom last night after service. I told her that I wanted to move away from Santa Clara. She asked why and I told her that I wanted to quit doing drugs and didn't feel like I could if I stayed there. She told me that she would see what she could do. It's a start. At least I have a plan. Only one more day of camp. That sucks and I am scared! I'm scared to fail again. Scared to go home, scared to go back to the hell I live in.

June 26
Dear Diary,

You will never believe what happened at the campfire tonight. People were standing up saying what they were thankful for or what the week had meant to them. Jude stood up and said he wanted to apologize to me, Caitlin, and Gwen. What the heck does that mean? Does that mean he messed around with them too? Man, what a mess. What the heck is his problem? I feel so stupid now. Caitlin and Gwen don't seem to have a clue what he is talking about. Are we all just hiding the same thing or do they really not have a clue?

Anyway, his apology was a huge surprise to me. I felt so embarrassed, like everyone knew what he meant, but that is just me. How can anyone know? I just have a guilty conscience about the whole messed-up affair. When will I ever stop feeling guilty about everything? He is the one that started everything. I never asked for his attention. This is the last thing I need to think about right now. I need to concentrate on making good decisions, not playing his stupid little games.

June 27
Dear Diary,

Home today. The van ride home was fun, but sad and scary. I wondered how my mom would act when I got home. We stopped at Dairy Queen. I didn't know what Dairy Queen was. I'd never been there before. I got an ice cream cone. It was so good. When I got home, I was in for a big surprise. Mom told me to get packing because we would move to Pleasanton at the end of the summer. I was so shocked, but so happy at the same time. So maybe things really can change now? Do I dare hope?

My Prayer

Lord, I want to thank you for everything. I really don't know what this world would be like if we didn't have you. I can't comprehend or even begin to. If your Son didn't die on the cross for us, there would be no hope.

So . . . thank you, Lord. Praise your name. This week I made so many decisions and commitments. I know I can only keep them with your help, Lord. I'm glad Jesus is coming for us soon. This here world is getting bad, but I know there is worse to come. Just help me to remember to pray for guidance, discipline, and obedience so I can get through until you send your son, Jesus, for us. Lord, I just want to do your will. Here am I Lord . . . send me. Help me to know through your Word what you want and give me strength. Amen.

July 20
Dear Diary,

  It has been a busy month. I have been all packed and ready to go for a week now. I haven't slipped at all as far as drugs. The day after I got home the guys wanted to go get high and I said I didn't want to. They were like, "Yeah, every time you go to camp that happens. In a few days you will be begging for a joint." Well, it has been more than a month and I still haven't had any pot or anything else for that matter. Not that I haven't been tempted. It hasn't been easy or anything, but I am staying strong. I have been going to church as much as I can. That is the worst part about moving. I will miss Grace so bad but Pleasanton is not that far away, we can visit and write and call. I won't miss Jude. He has been weird since camp. Whatever. I will miss Oskar too. We have had some good talks and he doesn't care that I have stopped doing drugs; he never bugs me about it and does not try to offer me any since I don't want it. He is awesome. Then there is Timothy, but he doesn't care anyway. I will miss him, but it will be easier to not see him all the time. I wonder if he knows . . .?

August 3
Dear Diary,

  We moved yesterday. I like the apartment and the area. It is pretty here. I am a little worried about going to a new school, but I will do fine. I am glad to have moved because it means Mom is trying to support me.

I am trying to do right. It isn't always easy, but like Monica told me, just start over again. I'm looking forward to starting all over where people don't know me. I can be anyone I want. There is no reputation to precede me, just whatever I want people to know. I can be little Miss Christian and no one will know any different.

There have been so many changes this year. I guess overall, I figured out that all of the stuff with my dad was not my fault. I don't need drugs to deal with all of the crap. My mom tries to help me the best way she knows how. I wish it was more, but I will be happy for what I have. I have to try to remember that she does the best she can. I have learned that I am not the world's biggest loser, druggie, slut. I have made mistakes, but I can overcome them. The most important thing I have learned is that God has a plan for my life. I don't know what it is or where it will take me, I just know that because of my life I will be able to help others. So, although my freshman year basically sucked, my summer turned things around and I think my sophomore year will be much better.

Epilogue

There is life after abuse. It takes a long time to unlearn the lessons of childhood and to replace them with the belief that I am valuable and precious in God's sight, that I have something to offer others. It is a journey and will continue to be a journey. Healing does not come instantly no matter how much I want it to.

Things with my mom went up and down throughout high school and my young adulthood. Children from abusive homes often look at one parent as the "good parent," especially when compared to a parent who overtly abuses. Next to my father, my mother was an okay mother. Through counseling, I was able to see the big picture more clearly. She wasn't the okay parent. To the contrary, my mother contributed to my abuse.

She sent me on visits with my father time after time. She sent me to live with my father on a full-time basis the summer after my sophomore year. He had a heart attack and "needed" someone to take care of him. I stayed for one day. On the first night, he called me over to the couch. He laid his head on my lap and pushed his nose into my crotch. I sat there in terror, all the old fears flooding through my body. Somehow, although I felt paralyzed by fear, I squirmed away, saying I had to go to the bathroom. I stayed in there with the shower running until I heard him go to bed.

In the middle of the night, he called me into his room. He said his heart was hurting and he needed help. I brought him his nitroglycerin pill and he asked me to put it in his mouth for him. He grabbed me and pulled me down. He started to kiss me and tried to pull into bed with him. He was stronger than I expected. He had me by my wrist and was forcing my hand down to his crotch. I pulled my arm and pushed away from him as hard as I could. I heard his head hit the headboard. I backed out of the room and locked myself in the bathroom. He kept crying out, "I'm dying. You're a terrible daughter. How can you be so mean and leave me here to die?" Then he switched tactics: "I love you so much. I need you with me. Please, come help me."

I spent the night curled up on the bathroom floor, shaking and crying, wondering if I really was killing him, if he really was having a heart attack, or if he was just trying to get me back in the room again so he could rape me. I didn't sleep at all. Every creak terrified me. I was on edge, waiting for him to come and break down the door to the bathroom. He never did.

After he left for work the next morning, I got dressed and repacked my bag. I called Timothy and asked him to please come and get me. He came, no questions asked, and brought me to Grace's. I asked her parents if I could stay there. They said that if my mom gave her permission, it would be fine with them.

I called my mom and told her that I'd run away. When she asked why, I told her, "He tried things again." I asked if I could just stay with Grace and she acquiesced. My mother said she'd talk to my dad about my leaving. Later, when I asked her what she said to my dad, she said, "I told him you went on vacation with a friend." She never told him the truth. I guess it was easier to lie. She was still tied to my father for financial reasons. She was unwilling to stand up for her children if it meant that she could no longer manipulate the situation to her advantage. So, she stayed silent, which in turn led to more shame and self-doubt for me.

I continued to turn to drugs and alcohol throughout high school to numb the pain of my life. My use was not as extensive as it was during my freshman year. I tried to live like a faithful Christian but often slid back into my self-destructive patterns. Because I had very little experience with faith and no support for my Christianity at home, it was difficult to maintain my fledgling faith. With the love and prayers of my friends, I made it through high school. I had survived, but I was still broken.

Two weeks after graduation, my mother told me to move out. I was only seventeen years old. I had recently quit my job, thinking I would move to California, but I had decided to stay in Arizona. I couldn't understand the reason I was being kicked out of the house. I obeyed the rules and tried to keep my anger to myself. I cleaned the house and worked thirty-two hours a week. I helped to pay the bills, and I bought all my own stuff when I was working. But her mind was made up. Two weeks later, I was in my own apartment with the first month paid courtesy of my mom. I found a full-time job and kissed my dream of going to college goodbye. Once I was out of my mother's house, I never did another drug, nor did I drink myself to oblivion. I didn't need it anymore. I did not make that correlation until years later.

Because of the abuse I was exposed to, my self-esteem was extremely low. Because of the lack of role models in my life, I did not know how to have a healthy relationship. My "saving" relationship turned into something neither of us wanted or expected. Mistakes were made on both ends.

At twenty-four years old, I found myself divorced with two small children. As a young single mom with two children, I found a strength I never knew I had. I had always been afraid to have children because I was told by many people that abused children abuse their children. I found that even during the stress of divorce, I could still be a mother who did not abuse her children.

I made mistakes—many of them. But I did not beat my children or neglect them or carry on patterns I had learned. I could overcome the statistics! During the hard times of my first marriage, I sought God, learned more about who he was and who he is through reading my Bible, questioning some of my belief systems, and reaching out to God in prayer. I still struggled with feelings of unworthiness to even call myself a Christian. I felt as if I would never be good enough. I did not yet understand the concept of grace. I just tried to hold on to the things I knew I was doing right, like being the best parent I could to my children. I read every parenting book I could get my hands on, and I watched how people I admired parented their children.

I remarried several years later to a man I had been friends with since my junior year in high school. After several years of marriage, I finally got the chance to go to college when I was thirty. I was both excited and terrified of returning to school.

During Psychology 101, Pavlov's experiment with dogs brought back strong memories of my father. My conditioned response was his bed, and I could not get those visions out of my head. The visions terrified me. I decided it was time to do something proactive. I went through group therapy specific to sexual abuse survivors to learn how to deal with the effects of the abuse.

It was by far the hardest thing I'd done up to that point in my life. It was the worst thing I had experienced because I started to relive those years as a child. My built-in survival mechanisms had blocked many memories from my childhood. I had huge gaps of time missing. Painful memories came out bit by bit. It was agonizing and heartbreaking. I often wondered how I would get through the pain of remembering.

Even though group therapy was a painful experience, it was there that I learned that everything I did, from the drugs to the sex, were all self-defense mechanisms. It was the only way I knew how to survive. I learned that survivors have very similar experiences and often cope with abuse in the same self-destructive ways. Therapy opened my eyes and began to loosen the grip of the guilt I had carried around for years. It helped me to realize that my reactions were normal for what I had been through.

I finished college and started teaching. I believed that teaching was one of the purposes that God had for me all those years ago when Reese told me, "Why not you?" God did indeed turn my situation into good. In my role as a teacher, I have been able to reach out and help students going through similar situations. Somehow, they know I will understand their pain. I believe I gained empathy I would not have had if not for my circumstances, and that allows me to connect with others who have experienced pain.

Part of the healing journey was to go back to therapy several times over the years. I was a part of several more group experiences and individual therapy. I had always known that I had been sexually abused; however, my memories of the actual abuse were limited. Over the years more detailed memories surfaced.

While in therapy with my last therapist, I knew I had gained skills and felt equipped to deal with the intensity of the memories. It was beyond difficult at times because each new memory revealed something worse than I had remembered before. I learned that the abuse began much earlier than I first remembered. Because the memories became worse with each new one that surfaced, I realized why they had been repressed for so long. The depravity of the acts my father committed against me grew in scope as I got older. I needed safety, support, and tools to be able to deal with that adequately.

I also realized that my mother had been verbally and physically abusive to me. When trying to get answers to questions as an adult, my mother refused to confirm details or take responsibility for her own abuse and her part in my father's abuse. I not only had memories of my father abusing me, but I also started to have memories of my mother abusing me. There were times in my childhood where my mother completely ignored any signs of abuse as well as allowing my father to beat us in front of her and even defending his actions.

Over the years, I attempted to have conversations with my mother and have some sort of relationship with her. Any mention of the abuse was met with denial. Due to this, I do not currently have a relationship with her. When I approached my mother with new information about the abuse, I requested a period of no communication in order to process what I had learned. I was tired of a relationship based on lies. I wanted to speak with her about the issues and had asked her to let me know when she was ready to talk about it. My mother simply never contacted me again. An ounce of truth destroyed a relationship that had been built on years of denial.

One thing that I did not initially tie to my abuse was health problems. I have suffered from headaches since I was a little girl, and those headaches became migraines by the time I was a teenager. With each passing year, the migraines became more frequent. I have been diagnosed with chronic migraines. I've had female problems for my entire life, including cysts, painful periods, heavy bleeding, miscarriages, and difficulty carrying pregnancies to term. I have also been diagnosed with fibromyalgia. Trauma research has found a strong correlation between health problems and childhood trauma.

During one period of therapy, when I was having more memories, it became important to me to find out as much information as I could regarding what happened when I was taken away and put in the shelter. The need to know, to have answers, and to find facts became almost an obsession. My therapist helped me to clarify my goals for finding concrete information, knowing that it could cause further pain. After many hours discussing the ins and outs and pros and cons, I decided to move forward in finding as many concrete answers as I could.

Researching any legal actions against my father was difficult, both in trying to get the records and then in reading the facts they contained. I started my research with the Child Welfare Information Gateway. I had to find out which city, and then which court, the trial was held. I had to search for police records and hospital records, some of which I was unable to find due to the time that had elapsed. I spent hours on the phone talking to social workers, court employees, hospital recordkeepers, and police investigators. I was asked multiple times if I was sure I wanted to know the information. I had to write letters and send requests for information. It was exhausting, and I was tempted to give up several times.

After obtaining the court records, I learned that my father was charged with four different felony counts: child molestation, child fornication, child oral copulation, and lewd and lascivious behavior involving a child. Only one count, lewd and lascivious behavior, stuck. He spent only ten months in jail and less than a year on probation. I cannot fathom how he got off so easily. It sickens me that all the charges did not stick and that he did not go to jail for life. He was absolutely guilty on all counts, and then some.

I do know that in the 1970s sexual abuse was still considered "a family issue" and it was not talked about. As an adult looking back, I am disappointed that Child Protective Services (CPS) and the psychiatric hospital did not recognize the severity of the abuse. I was not only failed by my parents, I was failed by the system—twice.

There were no follow-up visits from CPS after I went back home from the shelter. I will never understand why I was forced to return to my home. Although seeing the records in black and white was heartbreaking on so many levels, it answered questions for me that no one else would answer. I had thought perhaps I would find some sort of stipulation regarding my father's visitation rights. However, there were no restrictions on him other than to be employed and continue to see a counselor for as long as was deemed necessary. He saw a "counselor" for approximately six months. The counselor was associated with an organization that helped parents who had been "wrongly accused" of abuse. My father became the treasurer and bookkeeper for this organization less than a month after his release from jail. His punishment was barely a slap on the wrist. The consequences of his actions did not affect his ability to be gainfully employed nor did they stop him from his continued efforts to use me for his own benefit.

I know that I will continue to deal with abuse issues for the rest of my life; however, the abuse no longer rules over me. Painful memories will continue to reveal themselves. I know that there are a finite number of memories and that, one day, there will be nothing more to remember.

At times, I still struggle with shame over what happened to me. I struggle with the "good enough" concept and whether I am worthy. In most moments, I am secure in my relationship with God and I am comfortable with who I am. But sometimes, the fear returns out of nowhere, and I am thrust back into old thinking patterns and old fears. The difference is that I don't stay there.

I have learned to reach out to my support system. I have learned to reach out in prayer. I have learned that I am built of strong stuff and that, because I survived my childhood, I can survive anything. I have also learned that I am not only a survivor, but I am also an overcomer. If God can bring me healing, he can also bring healing to you. It takes hard work, friends, and faith. I have not arrived at completeness. I am a work in progress.

I taught for almost fifteen years. I was able to use my pain to help students from abusive families. Several years after earning my master's in education, God whispered to my heart that he wanted me to begin a new journey. With the support of my husband, family, and friends, I went back to graduate school and earned my degree in counseling.

The purpose to help others that was planted in my heart at summer camp my freshman year took on a new meaning. I have a unique insight into childhood trauma that I bring into the counseling session. My clients do not know my story, nor do they need to. What they do need is someone who can hold onto hope for them when they cannot hold onto it for themselves. They need someone who will validate them, normalize their choices and their fears, cheerlead their accomplishments, hold their hand through the darkness, and listen as they slowly and painfully reveal their stories. I am honored by their courage and perseverance as they work through the abuse they have experienced. I am thankful that my journey has allowed me to help others in their paths toward healing.

I will continue to grow and learn. I pray that God uses me to bring others the comfort with which I have been comforted (2 Corinthians 1:4–5). The journey to heal from childhood abuse is a long and difficult road. Sometimes I know exactly where I am; other times I feel hopelessly lost. During those times when I feel lost, I turn to the One who has led me on this journey. He has not failed me. God brought people into my life to help me on my journey, people I didn't realize until years later were there because of God's mercy. My prayer for those who have suffered at the hands of those called to love them is this: I pray you will come to know that God loves you. He will not fail or betray you. He knows your suffering. He felt it on the cross. He loves you, and it is unlike any love you have ever known.

From the Trenches

In compiling this section, my hope is to provide the reader with a look into some of the barriers and pitfalls of healing from childhood abuse, as well as to highlight what's helpful on this journey. Each section is written by the person identified: me, my husband Lance Turner, and my therapist Donna Price LMFT.

From the Author

Perhaps a better title for this section would be "What I wish I had known." Healing from childhood abuse is a long and difficult journey. Current research into trauma therapy says that it takes anywhere between three to five years of intense therapy to start to unravel the damage of abuse. The effects of childhood sexual abuse are insidious and far-reaching.

As an adult going through therapy, I saw that I had been failed by different systems: the schools, the court, Child Protective Services, the hospital, and my early therapy experiences. I am aware that when I was a child and adolescent, child abuse was still very much "a family matter" and it was thought that the best place for children was with a parent. Trauma therapy was in its infancy, and there was very little literature to guide professionals at that time. I'd like to say things have changed; however, the reality is that not much has changed.

Abused children are still sent back to live with their family, or they are re-traumatized in a poorly vetted placement situation. Childhood trauma is viewed as an exception. The magnitude of the problem is still unacknowledged and hidden in the shadows. This both saddens and angers me.

When I first began to address the abuse, I didn't know what I needed, how hard it would be, or how long it would take. If I had, I would have been completely overwhelmed; however, I would have also understood that the problems I experienced had a direct correlation to the abuse and I may not have been as hard on myself.

In this journey of healing from childhood abuse, I have worked with several different counselors. When I was a teenager, my first counselor showed me glimpses into a family dynamic where I began to see that my mother was a part of the problem. Because my counselor had to speak with my mother, she saw firsthand how my mother placed the blame for everything squarely on my shoulders.

During my first session, I remember catching a look of total disgust on my counselor's face as she followed my mother into the waiting room to get me. I was both surprised and hopeful after seeing that look, which I'm sure she did not mean for me to see. She told me, "Your mother is wrong. None of this is your fault, and you didn't try to kill yourself just to get attention. You didn't do that." It was what I needed to hear, especially after the hospital had ignored my requests to be sent to a foster home.

Psychotropic medication was still fairly new in the early 1980s and, being only fourteen years old, I took the advice of my therapist and the hospital psychiatrist and took the prescribed medication. I falsely believed that a pill would take away the blackness, and I think my therapist hoped it would ease some of the pain. I believe that she did the best she could with the limited understanding of childhood trauma that was available at that time. She planted a seed of understanding that my father was not the only one who abused me. At fourteen, that was empowering in some respects. On the other hand, to survive in that home, I had to forget that my mother was abusive.

My second therapy experience, in the abuse group I attended when I was thirty, opened my eyes to the many things that appeared unrelated but were a direct link to the abuse. I learned that many abuse survivors share common experiences: nightmares, gaps in memory, unexplained terror, substance abuse, promiscuity, abusive relationships, and depression. I learned (but didn't believe) that it wasn't my fault. I learned that I still had to keep secrets and that when I tried to broach the subject with my mother or sister, I was met with dismissal, stony silence, or blame. I learned that I "needed" antidepressants to survive because that's all I would ever do: survive. I learned that I was a survivor, and it was a label that identified me for the next decade. I learned that I couldn't trust anyone. I learned that the secrets I shared in that room had to stay in that room and could not be uttered outside those walls. I learned that writing helped me process the confusion I was feeling, but with nowhere for the confusion to go, it simply languished on paper and didn't help me make sense of the variety of ways the abuse had shaped my life.

Although the group experience was helpful in many ways, it was also harmful. The counselor who led the group was grounded in feminist theory. She dismissed my faith and did not make it safe for me to discuss any aspect of my faith within the group. She promoted inner strength and depending on oneself to power through the effects of the trauma, such as nightmares, depression, and difficulty being intimate with my spouse. She did not explain the risks of trauma therapy or what we could expect as we tried to untangle our stories. In a group of eight women, four dropped out. Several times, women were shut down in some aspect of telling their story. For example, if someone asked how their spouse could help them, she said, "Your spouse can't help with this. Don't tell them anything." The group members were led to believe that it would further damage our relationships if we tried to speak to our spouses about the abuse.

The antidepressant medication I took made me a shell of myself. I either felt totally numb or totally overwhelmed with darkness. While I was in group therapy, my husband planned a really nice dinner date for our anniversary. It was a huge treat to hire a babysitter and get dressed up to go to a fancy restaurant. I couldn't eat the meal and ended up in tears. All I could say was, "I ruined our dinner." I didn't know the medication had dulled my appetite as well as my mood.

I was unable to have sex with my husband for months at a time. The group leader's advice regarding sex was to tell our spouses/partners to "leave you alone until you are ready. You have to take back your power, and you never have to have sex again if you don't want to." I loved my husband and desired to have the same sexual relationship we'd had prior to therapy.

However, more often than not, when I tried to engage in sexual relations with him, I had flashbacks. I would either freeze up or power through, neither of which helped. Neither my husband nor I knew how to break those barriers. The only advice I was given was to have him read the book Ghosts in the Bedroom, which brought limited understanding.

About a year after completing group therapy, I began to have nightmares again. I wanted to see the same counselor on an individual basis so I wouldn't have to tell the whole story over again. She had moved to a different city, and we drove for over an hour to get to her new office. After explaining that the nightmares were back and that I didn't know what to do, she simply told me, "You aren't using the skills you learned. You need to power through the nightmares, and they will go away." I left her office feeling ashamed and like a failure because I couldn't control the ever-increasing nightmares.

Several years later, we moved to the mountains, something we'd been dreaming about for years. Although I loved where we were living, it was extremely stressful. My husband stayed behind to sell the house and continue working until he could find a job in our new town. I was in a new environment with a new job and no support system. My twelve-year-old son stayed in the city with his father. My fifteen-year-old daughter and three-year-old son lived with me.

My last counseling experience had made me leery of seeking out a new counselor. The extra stressors brought the nightmares roaring back. I also began to experience bits and pieces of memories that scared me to death. I had no idea if they were real or figments of my imagination. I seriously thought I was losing my mind. I had no idea that I was experiencing symptoms of post-traumatic stress disorder (PTSD). No one had ever explained that childhood trauma leaves a wide swath of symptoms in its path.

I was jumpy and always on edge. I was scared all the time. I was uncharacteristically irritable. In addition, I had a medically necessary hysterectomy right before the move. The surgery left me with a hole between my bladder and vaginal wall, which meant that I constantly leaked urine. I had linked my many "female problems" to my father's abuse, and so the surgery and subsequent complications brought everything to the surface.

I started to read through old journals and poems I had written during high school. I started to form those writings into the beginning of this story. Because my husband only came up on weekends, I often stayed up late into the night grading papers and then reading and writing. I was exhausted; however, I was too scared to sleep because when the nightmares came, there was no one there to comfort me and no escape from the pictures in my head that didn't end when I woke up screaming.

When my husband did come "home" for the weekends, he found what must have been a shell of his wife. All he saw was the stress and none of the happiness that he expected to see from a move to our dream town. He was confused by my stress and, because of the surgery complications, I felt dirty and disgusting when we had sex, which only contributed to building a distance between us.

I didn't tell him about the increase in nightmares and memories for several reasons. I thought I was crazy and that I should have "gotten over it" by now. It was ingrained in me that I couldn't tell him any specifics because he wouldn't understand. He would think I was disgusting and blame me if he really knew, and I had to protect him from the brutal truth of my life. It was a disaster waiting to happen.

Looking back, I can see that my husband was just as lost and confused as I was. The result is that we both retreated to our own inner worlds. I continued to write. Thinking that was the cause of my retreat, he would get upset with me and tell me to quit writing. I would get further frustrated and feel he could never possibly understand, which made me more certain that I could not share anything regarding the abuse with him.

One time, I tried to share by asking him to read some of what I had written. Unfortunately, much of what he read was related to my early promiscuity (another common factor in childhood sexual abuse), and he said, "I don't want to read about all your old boyfriends." That door was firmly shut.

During the next few years, I experienced a severe episode of depression. I continued to work and tried to be a good wife and mother. I felt that I failed at everything because I was unable to get myself out of the depression. I constantly had suicidal thoughts, and I felt like I couldn't tell anyone. My husband had no idea how to help, and I think he was scared of saying the wrong thing so he didn't say anything at all. I continued to write to try to process my internal world in the only way I knew how. The PTSD and depression symptoms eventually faded, and I tried to get back to living my life by ignoring my past.

Three years later, we moved again, this time to a different state. Our marriage was teetering, and the only thing that held it together was our stubbornness. Before getting married, we made a promise that we would never use the "D" word. That was the glue that held our marriage together.

About six months after moving, we found a church and started attending periodically. Due to the stressors of the move and another new job, I again began to experience symptoms such as an increase in nightmares, flashbacks, avoiding sleep, being on edge, irritability, and depression. I went to my doctor and got back on anti-depressants because that's what I was supposed to do when I was depressed. I had used anti-depressant medication each time memories started rising to the surface. I never had a physician tell me that anti-depressants are only a part of treatment and that I needed to be in therapy as well as taking medication.

Medication is a very personal decision between the individual, their doctor, and their therapist. In looking back on my experience with medication, I believe that I may have done better without it in the long run. The physical side effects were many, and weaning myself off anti-depressants "when I was better" was a horrible process. For me, the emotional side effects were worse. I was numb and I lost myself. If the anti-depressants worked, I don't believe I would have been suicidal or that I would have had such severe episodes of depression. My doctors needed to tell me that a pill would not "fix it," but rather that these pills were to be used in conjunction with therapy.

About a year after we had moved, I heard about a sexual abuse survivors group at church and decided to attend. The first night was my fortieth birthday, and I had determined that dealing with this "once and for all" was a good birthday present to give myself. The group was called Wounded Hearts, after the book The Wounded Heart.

In the second group meeting, we had to tell our story. When it was my turn, I said, "I was sexually abused by my father from my earliest memories until I was a teenager. He also beat me. My mom abused me too. It doesn't affect me much. I want to learn how to not have nightmares anymore."

I stated it as facts, with no emotion involved. Little did I know that that was the beginning of true healing. The group facilitator was gentle with the group members. She did not shame anyone for asking questions or bringing something up about their spouse. She talked about building a support system and telling others our story. She brought childhood sexual abuse out of the shadows and into the light. She talked about asking God to help us with whatever it was we were dealing with.

I completed the group and then rejoined it a few months later when it started over. I felt like I needed more. The second time I was in the group, I said something one night about my kids. The leader said, "I didn't even know you had kids." She had known me for about six months, and I had never mentioned my kids. I realized just how closed off I really was and how I held everything inside. I realized that was an effect of my childhood: don't talk, don't share, and don't let anyone know anything about you. It was deeply ingrained. I love being a mom, and it shocked me to my core that something that was so important to me was hidden from view.

She pulled me aside after the meeting and said, "We have a biblical counseling program, and I'm one of the counselors. I think you could use some one-on-one. Would you like to do that?" I agreed and started seeing her individually.

In every counseling session, we prayed about what I was experiencing. She noticed when I would start to pull away and hide, and she wouldn't let me. She broke the walls that held back the tears and, for the first time, I really allowed myself to cry and heal. I worked with her for many months, and I eventually went on to co-lead and then later lead the group. It was during my counseling with my group leader that my husband and I decided we needed to see a therapist about our marriage. We could no longer do it on our own.

We were referred to a new therapist for marital therapy. A few months into therapy, problems with sexual intimacy came up. I explained that when I was "dealing with childhood stuff," sex was off the table. My therapist told us that my childhood sexual abuse directly affected our sex life and our marriage. She discussed her belief that I wasn't "over it," and that until I dealt directly with the abuse, it would continue to affect our marriage and our lives.

My husband and I agreed to take a break from marriage counseling and, once again, I started individual therapy for childhood sexual abuse. One of the first helpful things my therapist did was to educate me on PTSD and depression and the link to childhood sexual abuse. She encouraged me to share as much as I could with my husband because keeping him out of that part of my life was putting us on different teams. She taught me techniques such as the container technique and grounding that I could use when the flashbacks and nightmares became overwhelming. She encouraged me to use whatever supports I had available, including my faith, my husband, and reaching out to friends. She encouraged me to continue writing.

During one session, I told her that I had written about the abuse in story form and asked her if she would read it. I hoped that it would be easier for me than trying to tell her everything. She agreed, and I brought in the story I'd been writing off and on over the past eight years. After she read my story and didn't turn away in horror from me— which was what I expected—I began to disclose bits and pieces of the details I was remembering.

I shared with her about the nightmares where I woke up screaming. The nightmares turned into flashbacks, which felt as if everything was happening in that moment. It was like watching a movie of myself and the things that were happening to me as a child.

Once, during a particularly difficult session, I brought up how much my stomach hurt and that it had been hurting for weeks with no apparent cause. My therapist explained body memories: the body holds on to what happened during trauma. She taught me not to fear the memories. "Look at them as yourself telling yourself that you're in a safe place and you're strong enough to deal with whatever is behind the nightmares and the memories." The words started to tumble out of me as my therapist encouraged me. "Use your voice. It was stolen from you. You weren't allowed to speak about anything or say how you felt. You can use your voice and your words because you are safe now." Each time I revealed some new aspect of the trauma, I was met with kindness, understanding, and reassurance.

My therapist helped me explore what I had told her. Growing up in my home, abuse was normal. I had an idea of what a healthy family looked like because I had spent so much time with my best friend's family. However, I still struggled with understanding just how abusive my mother had been. By reflecting back my own words, my counselor helped expose the ways that my mother was abusive, how the youth pastor took advantage of and abused me, and how the multiple systems that I'd had contact with had let me down. My counselor displayed her anger over the many times I was failed, which helped me understand that my "normal" was, at best, horrible.

Through the months of therapy, I learned that the more I opened up, the more I remembered. My therapist never asked me leading questions. She simply gave me tools and made the room a safe space to talk about the horrors

I had experienced. I felt like she was truly invested in my healing.

She asked if I wanted to try Eye Movement Desensitization and Reprocessing (EMDR) therapy. I researched the therapy and learned about its risks and benefits. I talked to my friends and my husband about it and decided to begin EMDR. In this therapy, we began with a detailed memory. Sometimes we would begin with a pain in my body, and when we focused on that pain, the memories would come flooding back. I remembered things I wish I could have forgotten. I left each session feeling utterly exhausted.

However, I also felt a sense of hope that these memories that had haunted me for years were finally being addressed in a way that would bring resolution. Although it was painful and exhausting work, I could see results. If we started with a body memory, the physical pain would generally be resolved. I had information, and I would grieve the loss from what I had experienced. I was able to see myself from a compassionate perspective instead of seeing myself as the enemy.

I felt sadness, horror, anger, disgust, and disbelief. But I no longer felt the intense and pervading fear that had haunted me my entire life. After every session, my therapist told me how brave and how strong I was and how much resilience I had. She pointed out my many strengths, and I slowly began to believe her. She helped me untangle lies from truth. She helped me build a strong support system and then, when I was ready, she helped me include my husband.

I still feared sharing details with my husband. During this period of therapy, he was still in the dark about the intensity of what I was walking through. I told him I had a flashback or memory of something "awful," and it would stop there.

One day, while praying, I had a strong sense that God wanted me to share details of a particular traumatic memory with my husband. I talked to my therapist about it and she helped me develop a game plan. We'd been back in couples counseling and were working on team-building. I felt like God was telling me that revealing some details of the abuse to him would help us to build our team.

I wrote out one of the memories and we went to a park. We sat on the bleachers. I pulled out the paper and began to read what I had written. I rarely cried in front of my husband, but I could not stop the tears from flowing as I read. He sat beside me, letting me finish. I couldn't look at him while I was reading. When I was done, we sat in silence. I felt an overwhelming sense of shame as well as fear that he would reject me. I can't remember who spoke first.

What I do remember is that he said, "I never knew. No wonder why it's been so hard. I'm sorry." That moment was the beginning of a much deeper relationship with my husband.

I'd like to believe that if my first therapist had been a good fit for me, my husband and I would not have had such a difficult time. It's not that we would never have had problems. It's just that now we are on the same team, a team that works together to rebuild and redeem what was stolen from me. My husband has an incredibly strong, protective spirit, and by shutting him out I shut out the one thing that I needed the most: someone to protect me and keep me safe. And I shut out his ability to use his strength for the good of our marriage. I realized that even though

I had shut him out, his constant presence allowed me the room to reach out, to engage in therapy over the course of many years, and to strive after healing.

There were so many things that could have made the journey easier for me and for my family, like being educated about the effects of childhood abuse, being guided to build a support system rather than depending on inner strength, having someone who looked at the whole system rather than just at the symptoms as they showed up, and having my faith included as a part of my healing journey. Those things promoted healing.

If I had begun my therapy journey with my last therapist, I wonder if the journey would have been so difficult. In my first group experience, I had the expectation that I would "be all better." That was hardly the case, and that expectation, which was reinforced when I sought her help again, led me to believe that I was broken beyond repair and something inside of me was deeply flawed. I was led to believe that I just needed to be strong and I needed to depend on the fact that I was a survivor. I had survived the initial abuse; thus, I could survive anything. There was no talk of ongoing symptoms or effects, no discussion of the lasting impacts, and no roadmap to follow. I don't blame the therapist. I believe that she did the best she could with what she had. However, it was damaging to have those false expectations. It's important for people to understand that just because someone is a therapist, it does not mean they are equipped to deal with childhood trauma, or that they are a good fit for you personally. I wish I had known that. I didn't know what I was missing until I began working with a therapist who wasn't afraid of my story or of walking through the shadows with me.

People often ask, "How did you overcome your childhood?"

As a therapist, I ask myself, "What do my clients have that leads to their ability to be resilient?"

It's a chicken-or-egg question. My ability to thrive, rather than just survive, is directly due to a caring therapist who had experience working with childhood trauma. I can't express the importance of finding a therapist whom you feel safe with, who allows you to tell your story at your pace, and whom you feel is committed to helping you through childhood trauma. I also know that for myself, as well as what I've seen in therapy and read in the research, a support network is critical to healing.

My support network was something I intentionally pursued. After years of doing it by myself, I purposefully began to build a friendship with two women who shared similar values. I knew they would not advise me to shift blame to someone else without owning my own stuff. I knew they would push me to be the best me possible. It took time to build that trust, but, eventually, I began to take real risks in disclosing some of what I was walking through in therapy.

They allowed me space to process. When my thinking was based on shame and self-blame, they would gently correct me. When my thinking was based on blaming others, they helped me to look at my part, the only thing that I had control over. They challenged me to overcome the addiction of perfectionism. They helped me to pray when I didn't have words. They met me with love and understanding every step of the way. I learned that I did not have to carry my burdens by myself, and I learned that there is freedom in allowing others to truly help me through the dark places. I learned that the risk of being vulnerable is worth being deeply known and loved. Through these women, I started to see my value, and I started the hard process of learning to love myself.

It may seem strange that I allowed my friends into the process of healing before my husband. In looking at that aspect of my journey, I know that is because I was afraid that if my husband really knew, he would leave me. It took years to begin including my husband in the details. Neither of us knew what the heck we were doing, and both of us had gotten bad advice. My husband was afraid of causing further damage so he isolated himself. I was afraid that including him would further damage our sometimes-tenuous relationship, so I isolated myself. Reading what I had written to him was one of the most difficult things I had ever done. I had no idea how he would react. What I did know was that God wouldn't ask me to do something that would harm me. My husband and I know that moment was the turning point in our relationship. For me, I was able to finally accept the safety that had been there all along. Telling him broke the secrecy, and it completely broke the belief that I had to do it alone.

The most important thing for me was to bring my faith directly into the middle of the worst messes from the trauma. I had to ask hard questions like, "Where were you God?" and I had to be open to any answers. I had to talk to God in a very vulnerable and real way. My prayer time was ugly and messy in the midst of the worse parts of the trauma therapy. I learned that I could be angry with God and question his motives and his very existence without losing my faith. I learned that the difficulty in healing from childhood trauma was not a failing of my faith but rather a failing of people. I learned to forgive the things that had been done to me and the things that I had done as a result.

I learned that forgiveness isn't a "one and done" but rather a process that unfolds slowly.

Each time something new arose, I needed to walk through the steps of processing my emotions and thoughts in order to forgive. Through wrestling with God, I learned to trust that he did not want this to happen to me and that it broke his heart. I learned that he was there in the midst of my worst pain. I learned that he was dependable and that I could ask him anything. The process of building my faith was long and difficult and would not have been possible without people who were "Jesus with skin on" for me. They helped show me who God is and how to turn to him for everything, not just the safe things. My faith has helped me turn the mess into a message of hope. Those things have made all the difference on this journey.

From the Spouse
by Lance Turner

When my wife first told me that she had been sexually abused, she said it casually: "Hey, my dad sexually abused me, but I'm okay." Because I didn't know anything about sexual abuse and because she said it wasn't a big deal, I thought everything was okay. She acted like it didn't affect her at all when she told me about the abuse. The first couple of years of being married were pretty normal, and the abuse didn't seem to impact our relationship. I think that she started to get triggered from her psychology class, and, because of that, she started remembering, and she was unable to shut the memories down.

After she told me about the abuse, it explained some things from when we were in high school. She did this push/pull thing where she acted like she wanted a relationship and then she pulled away. Years later, she was able to explain that, during high school, she thought I was too nice. Because she felt bad about herself, she didn't think she could be with someone who was nice and treated her well.

When we got together as adults, she was going through a divorce. We were both really confused because she had all these very mixed feelings. It wasn't until after years of therapy that she was able to make the connection to the divorce triggering stuff from her childhood. At the time, I didn't know how to deal with her confusion, and I didn't handle it very well.

If someone had told me that their fiancée had been sexually abused, I would tell them it's probably a much bigger deal than they think it is. I'd tell them to be skeptical of their fiancée believing it's not a problem because they have probably spent years hiding from the impact. I'd suggest they attend counseling together before going any further. It's not that the person who was abused is lying; they just don't know.

When my wife and I got married, it was her normal. She didn't have a clue. There was no way for her to tell me, "Hey, I had this thing happen, and it's a problem." At the beginning of our marriage, we thought "Okay, this thing happened" rather than "Holy crap! This is a really horrible thing that happened, and I'm totally screwed up from it."

The first time my wife went to counseling, we'd been married for four years. I thought she just needed to hear, "Yeah, it's okay" versus going to years of therapy. I thought therapy would make her all better. It would have been good if I'd been involved in therapy at that point. Then I would have been able to see up close and personal, "Okay, this isn't a bandage thing. This is something that needs to be worked on." I would have realized that she couldn't just go to therapy for a little while and be fixed.

When she went to a group therapy session, she'd come back out of sorts and out of whack. I wouldn't know how to calm her down. I didn't know how to treat her. I didn't know anything about what was going on with her. I felt like I couldn't relate to her anymore. I needed to know why she felt the need to isolate, and I needed a lot more information on triggers because it was a crapshoot. She'd get mad, and I wouldn't know why. Now I know she was being triggered, but I couldn't see it then. All I could see was that she was mad at me. I didn't know she was coming from a different direction. And at the time, she couldn't explain it because she didn't know what was triggering her or even that she was being triggered.

If I could do it over, I would have asked to go to therapy with her so that I would have had a better idea of what was going on and why she was angry all the time. It felt like she was just mad at me. She'd tell me that I'd done the same thing as someone else had done to her in the past. I thought, "Okay, now you're just mad at me because I'm me." I didn't know what was going on with my wife, so I took everything personally. Now, I know I can ask her questions to get some clarification when she's upset.

It was confusing to me that after she started therapy, she was different. She had her personality, and then—boom—she was a different person. She was a lot angrier. She isolated more. It was almost like she wasn't there anymore. I felt like she didn't care about me. She was just glad that someone was there to help take care of the kids while she was wrapped up in her own stuff. It was hard because I didn't understand what was happening or where my wife went. I just knew everything was totally different.

Even though she wasn't mad at me per se, she was just mad at the whole thing. I felt like the best thing to do was just let her do her thing and stay out of her way. It made it worse when I retreated. I should have stayed involved with her and her therapy. I should have found somebody else to talk to about the situation. It would have helped me to deal with feeling rejected because she wasn't rejecting me on purpose. Looking back, I'd say the anger and isolation were signs of a problem.

There were times when she was melancholy for no reason I could see. I was thinking, "Everything's fine. What the heck?" She didn't have a bad day at work, but something would happen that would set her off. I didn't know what to do when she was depressed. To me, it felt like she was depressed because of our marriage. If I'd known then what I know now, I would have been able to say, "Okay, something happened that made her go back to that time and made it real for her again."

Things happened that didn't make sense, like "Why does [insert random thing here] make her crazy?" Something we didn't know at the time was that the prescribed drugs were really just a bandage. Unfortunately, that medication didn't help. It merely hid my wife and made her numb. The person I'd known went away. We thought the medication would make her better, but it didn't. She needed trauma therapy, not a bandage.

At that point, we both needed to talk to a counselor who understood trauma. We needed information about possible repercussions from sexual abuse and how to minimize any problems. And I should have seen a counselor individually. Then I would have known what to look for. I would have known that withdrawal and isolation, problems with getting and staying close to your partner, and an unwillingness to talk about the abuse are common signs. After years of therapy and working on this, we know that even though she thought she had dealt with it, she really hadn't. Most people who have dealt with childhood abuse well enough to adjust are willing to talk about it.

I want to emphasize the importance of a counselor who

understands that the abuse isn't just affecting the individual; it's affecting their whole family. The first counselor my wife had set us back. My wife had made a breakthrough of, "Okay, there's a problem here that I need to figure out." I was all for that. That counselor didn't have any practical advice for my wife on how to approach me. It did squat for our relationship. It brought more information out for my wife, but it didn't help me in any way.

She would come home from therapy and tell me that the counselor said abuse was all the fault of men, and it seemed like she hated men. She didn't help my wife learn to adjust to me or to point out that some things are just normal for men and have nothing to do with being an abusive jerk. The counselor should have said, "Okay Kimberly, why don't you step out?" and then had me come in and say, "Okay, here's what's happening. Here's what you can look for. Here are some signs." It would've helped me understand her and not try to fix her or get her out of a mood. It would have helped me recognize that whatever was going on for her wasn't directed toward me. There was none of that.

The message I got was, "Hey, asshole, don't make it worse." The only thing the counselor offered to spouses was to read the book Ghosts in the Bedroom. It helped a little, but I would have preferred having someone explain it to me so I could ask questions. The book was too focused in some ways. It focused on issues with sex, but first you have to get to the bedroom. At that time, she wasn't able to get to that point. I needed advice on how to get through each day.

A few years after her first therapy sessions, we moved to a new town. My wife started to write about the abuse, and I felt like all that did was bring up a bunch of crap and upset her. I didn't understand that she was trying to make sense of what was going on for her at that time. She didn't have a counselor who could have helped her deal with what was coming up in her writing. I probably should have said, "This is affecting us, and we should we figure this out together," but I had no clue at the time. We'd moved to our dream town. We both had jobs. We were fine. I thought, "Things are good. Why is she depressed?"

I didn't know that change, good or bad, is a stressor that might trigger PTSD symptoms. And she didn't know she had PTSD. Her first counselor only talked about depression with her. I knew she was dealing with something, but I wasn't included. I was flying blind. It was frustrating because I couldn't help her.

Looking back, I can see the triggers: "Oh, she's feeling stressed because of the move and new job. The stress is bringing up this other stuff." It didn't occur to me at the time. I thought, "What's wrong with this? What's going on day to day that she's feeling so bad about?" I didn't get it. She liked her job, and she liked where we were living. It was frustrating because, even if I had been trying to fix her, I would have at least had some clue as to why I couldn't get her fixed. Now we recognize that a lot of the stuff she was experiencing was related to PTSD. If I had known the common signs, I would have thought, "She's dealing with what happened back then, and she has no control of that. And I don't have any control of it. It's a matter of us getting through it together."

When my wife started seeing a good therapist, I still didn't know what was going on for her. I didn't know to what extent she had dealt with stuff. I didn't know how she was seeing things. I had no idea what sexual abuse meant for her. It could have been one time somebody touched her versus what really happened, which was a completely different thing. There's a spectrum there.

When she began to include me, we talked about issues that were frustrating for both of us. She began to tell me specifics. Before she shared with me, I thought that her dad had done some "thing" to her maybe once or twice. But I didn't know what the "thing" was. After she began to tell me about the abuse, I felt like she had really suffered, and I understood that it had been long-term. It wasn't like she could talk about one event, deal with it, and get it out of her system. Multiple events had happened over multiple years. She didn't have this one memory that she could just take care of; she kept having new ones adding to everything.

When she shared some of the memories, it made it more real. I knew that it was something she didn't even know the extent of, and her memories were getting deeper and worse all the time. Early on, the only nightmare she ever told me about was someone was chasing her, so I thought, "Okay, it's one thing. It wasn't ten different things." I thought that if she had the same nightmare every time, she should be able to work through that, figure it out, and put it aside, right? I thought, "Okay she's having a nightmare. I have nightmares. I don't even remember them when I wake up." I couldn't understand why it was so hard.

It wasn't until she started sharing memories with me that I realized it could be a different memory every time. It would have helped me if someone had told me, "Hey, you know, she's probably having flashbacks, not nightmares. That's different." People need to know the difference between nightmares and flashbacks. You can have flashbacks during the day or after a nightmare. That flashback can make all the difference in how someone is feeling. Something we never understood clearly was that it wasn't just the sexual abuse and her dad beating her that she was dealing with. She also ended up with this abuse from her mom that made it worse. She didn't have anybody to support her.

When we went back to marriage therapy, that was the point where I knew this was not something to be fixed. I started to understand that our problems were not all my wife's fault and that our problems were not just her problems to solve. More or less, I came to terms with "this is the way it is, and I have to work on this myself." My thoughts went from "when she gets better, everything will be better" to "how can we do this together?" That changed when my wife started to explain what had happened to her.

Therapy helped us figure out that stress would bring up nightmares and then flashbacks, and then she'd just go down that road. I knew, "Okay, now she's upset. Now she's crying." I could see the progression, and I could see that "none of that is great, but it's not abnormal either." Once I had information, I understood that her reaction was completely expected. If we only would have known that twenty years ago. That's what's so frustrating. If she would have had a decent counselor from day one, I think at least half of our issues wouldn't have happened. She should have had a counselor at the beginning, when she first told someone, rather than having to wait until she thought she was losing her mind.

My wife didn't self-medicate with substances. She said that she'd done enough of that in high school. Because her father was an alcoholic, she worried about that for herself. One of the things that took us a long time to realize is that her form of self-medicating was perfectionism. She believed that if everything were in her control, she would be okay. When things got out of order, it was really hard for her. She was obsessive about organizing and cleaning, and she held herself to impossible standards of doing everything perfectly. She believed that if she did everything right, then she would be good enough. I just thought, "Oh, you're a perfectionist. Okay." When her symptoms were the worst, the perfectionism was detrimental to our family. None of us could live up to her standards. At the time, I didn't know that controlling things as an adult was linked to not being able to control anything as a child. Now I can see that the times the perfectionism was stronger was when she was having a lot of memories or we had a lot of changes in our lives.

The trauma didn't only affect my wife; it affected the whole family. She would withdraw and become angry. Sometimes, she just wasn't present. Other times, she would get super defensive and take out her frustrations on us. That led to us personalizing her anger because we didn't see what that trigger was. We assumed, "We are here, so it must be us." Years later, we figured out that when our daughter was six, it triggered stuff from when my wife was six, but she didn't even know it. Neither one of us were aware of anything until years down the road when we got a better therapist who explained that to us. It's obvious now, but it wasn't obvious then.

If I were going to give someone advice, I'd say the biggest thing I learned is not to take it personally. Find your way around that one, which is super difficult because it's hard to put aside, especially for men. We're more in the moment, so we think, "If you're upset and you're with me, you must be upset with me" versus, "You're thinking about something that happened thirty years ago." If I didn't take it personally, I wouldn't have isolated myself so much. I should have found friends and gone and done more friend stuff. I would have known there was nothing I could do to fix her or make her not be upset. I could have gone out with my friends to do something that helped my mood. I always felt like if my wife was feeling melancholy, I had to hang around so I could bring her out of it or do something that would cheer her up. She'd say, "Get away from me!" and I'd say, "I'm trying to be with you." We were both dealing with this thing we didn't understand. We thought the other person was the problem when it was really not their problem at all. Having supportive friends can help you deal with the frustration you feel.

My own counseling would have helped me if it was the right counselor. And that is the key, because if I had just gotten somebody who'd said, "Oh, don't worry about it," that would have been the same crap. You need somebody who is going to know what you're going through, someone who could say, "Yes, she might be mad because you did something, but that was a trigger. It was not you." I would have been able to express my frustration and figure out that what she was going through had nothing to do with me. If I had known about the real impact of abuse, I would have treated my wife differently. I would have tried to see things more her way. It's frustrating because I look back and think, "Well, I could have done this, or I could have done that." But because I didn't know what she was going through, I was unable to deal with the way she treated me.

The reason we made it through this is that we're both

stubborn. We didn't give up. The turning point was getting a good counselor because that first therapist in Phoenix was just terrible. She didn't help my wife, and she didn't help me. The marriage therapist saw that there was a problem. When we went in together, she recognized that the problems between us were actually related to the abuse rather than, "You two have problems."

It started to make more sense, and I had more understanding that the abuse was still back there, still pushing buttons, still affecting us. I just had to look at this as the new normal, period. There's never any going back to the way things were before. Several years after going to therapy, I had the opportunity to take a Mental Health First Aid USA™ class. Even though it wasn't directly applicable to our situation at that time, I believe the information I got and the strategies I learned would have been helpful earlier.

Some things I wish we had known in the beginning are:

If your spouse has been abused, it's a bigger deal than either of you think.

Learn as much as you can about common signs and behaviors for someone who has been abused. For my wife, it was depression and PTSD, but it could be other things.

Learn about helping people with mental health issues.

Have your own support system and don't personalize everything.

Try to be involved in her therapy, but don't push yourself in. It takes time.

Make sure the counselor is a good fit. If you want to have a good marriage and the counselor says to your wife, "All men are pigs," then that makes it hard.

The Author's Thoughts on Therapy - From Both Sides of the Couch

A good therapist is critical to helping one heal from childhood abuse. If you are not comfortable sharing freely with your therapist, it is okay to find a new one. My first therapist did not allow me to bring my faith into the counseling room. I wish I had realized that I could change counselors at that time. A safe therapy environment is created when you, as the client, feel supported, safe, and like you can share anything you need to talk about. If you feel like your counselor is not understanding or listening to you, talk to him or her. The counselor may simply need to try a different approach, and a good counselor will be flexible enough to change their style. If you still don't feel safe, find a different counselor.

It's important to begin skill-building before jumping directly into processing trauma. You should learn techniques to manage your emotions. For example, my counselor taught me to visualize a container that would hold all of my stuff between sessions, and I could revisit that container when memories intruded between sessions. She also taught me a skill called grounding, which helped bring me back to the present when I experienced flashbacks. Different counselors teach different skills. There are many ways to help you learn to regulate your emotional responses. The counselor simply needs to give you several tools to use when you are distressed, and they need to make sure that you are using them effectively before beginning any intense trauma processing.

In addition, the counselor should talk to you about your outside support system as well as making sure that your current environment is safe before beginning any trauma work. You need at least one safe person in your life. Your counselor may ask to speak with your safe person to help educate them about what you may be experiencing. The counselor will help you build safe and supportive relationships outside of the counseling room by talking to you about what makes someone safe, how to effectively communicate your needs, how to set and enforce boundaries, and how to find safe people for your support network.

Although I am a professional counselor, I wanted an outside perspective on what makes therapy effective as well as what a client might expect in trauma therapy. I enlisted the help of my personal therapist, who has years of trauma therapy experience, for this next section. It's written for both the client and the therapist. My hope is that it answers some questions for you as the reader and that you find the information helpful.

From (and for) the Therapist
by Donna Price, LMFT, retired

A helpful therapist is someone who listens well and has the expertise to address the issues which are presented by the client. Professional referrals and word of mouth are the best avenues for locating an experienced therapist. However, a good personal fit is equally important to the process of developing a therapeutic relationship. It is the client's responsibility to determine whether a therapist is suited to them. The best test of this is how safe the client feels in the first session or two. Trauma survivors are especially capable of making this determination due to their highly developed intuition regarding their own safety needs.

Most therapists have a process they go through when beginning therapy with a new client. Therapists routinely ask about abuse in the history-taking stage. If clients have not repressed the memory of abuse, and if they are ready to address the issue, they will usually disclose this information. It is best if the abuse can be verified by another party close to the client, but this is often not possible. However, it is not uncommon for the abuse history to surface during the process of therapy, either because the memories have been repressed or the client didn't feel safe enough to disclose it earlier. If the abuse is ongoing, it is the therapist's responsibility to assure the safety of the client immediately. This may involve legal action such as restraining orders and legally mandated reporting and notification of parents if the client is a minor.

Therapists should recognize the limitations of their training and expertise and should refer a client at the earliest point where they recognize the need. The longer the relationship continues, the harder it will be for the client to make the transition to a new therapist.

Once the abuse is identified, it is necessary for the client to process the abuse in some way. There is a huge difference between a client with a PTSD diagnosis and a Complex PTSD diagnosis. The latter applies to early and prolonged abuse of any kind, especially by a family member or other trusted person or multiple people, such as incest, ritual abuse, etc. The younger the initiation of the abuse, the more likely there will be neurological changes in the brain which will complicate treatment profoundly.

The treatment of choice for PTSD is Eye Movement Desensitization and Reprocessing (EMDR) because it is fast and minimizes time spent in processing the abuse. However, this may not be appropriate for clients with Complex PTSD due to the client's inability to distinguish between observing and reexperiencing the trauma. In these cases, Dialectical Behavioral Therapy (DBT) is the treatment which best addresses the emotion regulation and distress tolerance deficits from which these clients suffer.

Mindfulness practice, which is also taught in a DBT program, is the best technique for tolerating the disturbing intrusion of abuse memories which are common in PTSD survivors. The goal of therapy is not to forget the abuse but to remove the emotional charge the memories contain. By externalizing the experience of the abuse and assigning responsibility to the abuser, the client gets to see that the abuse was not their fault and that they did not deserve or provoke it in any way. At this point, the goal is to develop a positive and healthy self-image which can replace the shattered sense of self-efficacy which the abuse caused.

This is usually long-term work, especially in Complex PTSD survivors. It is also very individually driven and depends on the internal resources of the client and the motivation to recover. The initial stages can be excruciatingly slow and non-progressive, with lots of potential for coexisting conditions, including autoimmune disorders, addictions, eating disorders, unhealthy relationships, child abuse, and medical complications. This is difficult work. Therapists who are not intentional about self-care are vulnerable to burnout.

Individual survivors go through different stages depending on their circumstances, but a simplified representation of the process is: victim to survivor to overcomer. As a victim, they identify as hopeless and helpless over their recovery. This is usually manifested as either depression, anxiety, or both. They have not yet taken responsibility for their recovery and do not know how to change. The therapist's job is to bring the traumatic memories to the surface, address them, and assign responsibility to the perpetrator(s). This is the most painful stage and may cause client resistance for that reason. Clients need to recognize that burying the trauma has not served them and then find the courage to address it.

The survivor stage is where the client works on reconstructing a new persona. Individual client strengths are paramount in this process as they provide a starting point.

The work in this stage builds on existing strengths and develops new ones. A strong faith is a definite asset, especially in this area of the recovery process. It should be tapped into whenever the client is open to doing so.

The overcomer stage is where the client acknowledges the trauma without identifying with it. It no longer defines them but gives them a strength and purpose. Life changes are often made at this stage in the service of self and others. There will be scars from the abuse but no open wounds or festering boils. Ideally, forgiveness will be achieved toward the perpetrator(s) to complete the process of freeing the client from their own past hurts. Although reconciliation is rare, when it is in the client's best interest, the therapist may choose to facilitate that process.

A support system is critical to the client's ability to tolerate therapy for abuse. The supportive individuals should be identified initially, and the client should be encouraged to include them in the therapeutic process from the start of therapy. The therapist may get written releases to involve these individuals if and when the client agrees to include them. This is a very individually driven decision and must always be made in the best interest of the client's progress in therapy. A supportive significant other should be open to listening without fixing and should have healthy boundaries about his or her responsibility for self-care and the way in which the client wishes to be helped. The client needs to take the lead in expressing what the support should look like.

Never Alone

"And I pray that you, being rooted and established in love, may have power, together with all the Lord's holy people, to grasp how wide and long and high and deep is the love of Christ, and to know this love that surpasses knowledge—that you may be filled to the measure of all the fullness of God" (Ephesians 3:17–19).

How wide? Wide enough to cast a net of prayer over me that I never knew existed. About thirty years after the fact, I learned that several ladies in the church I had attended for the Day Camp had consistently prayed for me. They did not know my story; however, God laid me on their hearts and they prayed. I have no doubt that their prayer saved me from myself on many occasions.

How long? Long enough to heal from childhood trauma. God was with me on this journey, every step of the way. He placed people all along the path: a caring principal, a teacher that listened and acted, a kind police officer, a judge who broke my resolve to lie, a neighborhood babysitter who happened to be a Christian, a wise youth pastor who didn't pretend he had all the answers, a best friend and her family, and a boyfriend whose kindness and words of encouragement I turned to time and time again through the dark years. God was there in these people before I knew of his existence.

How high? High enough to bridge the gap between myself and God. People, who were Jesus with skin on, helped connect me to God: Joanna, Donna, Roy, Tammy, and Shelli.

How deep? Deeper than the depths of despair, deeper than the deepest valley, deeper than the hell I lived in. Lance, Whitney, Mitchell, and Marcus—you walked through the deep waters with me, and you would not let me drown. You held me up, many times unbeknownst to you. The depth of God's love for me is manifest in what I have learned from being your wife and your mama.

Acknowledgements

I want to thank my editor, Blake, for his work in cleaning up the manuscript. Shelli, thank you for endless hours going over syntax and word choice and helping me to re-organize sections to add clarity. I'd like to thank my publisher, Robert, for seeing something in my story that was worth pursuing and working with me on completing the manuscript so that it met my goal of helping others.

I want to thank my family for the many ways they have supported me on my journey toward healing from childhood trauma.

And most importantly, I want to thank God, without whom my story would not have been possible. There were so many times that God intersected my life, using circumstances and people, in ways that only could have been His hand. Those instances gave me a glimpse of hope, which was all I needed to keep moving forward. Everything I am is because of who He is.

Resource List

I have personally used and found these resources helpful in my own journey toward healing.

Dan Allender, The Wounded Heart: Hope for Adult Victims of Childhood Sexual Abuse (Colorado Springs: NavPress, 1990).

*This is the book that I used in my second group experience. It opened the way for including my faith in the healing process. There is a workbook that can be used as well. I would not recommend using this book by yourself, but rather in a group or with a therapist.

"Child Welfare Information Gateway," US Department of Health and Humans Services, https://www.childwelfare.gov.

*I used this website to begin my search for the children's shelter, Child Protective Services records, and which court had jurisdiction over my case.

Henry Cloud and John Townsend, Boundaries: When to Say Yes, How to Say No, to Take Control of Your Life (Grand Rapids: Zondervan, 1994).

*After going through the Wounded Hearts class several times, I took a boundaries class at my church. The class and the book were life changing. I had never heard of boundaries and I had no idea what a healthy boundary was or what it looked like. This book helped me to redefine myself as an individual who has the right to my own thoughts, feelings, and desires. It was pivotal in helping me to make changes in all of my relationships.

Mary DeMuth, Not Marked: Finding Hope and Healing After Sexual Abuse (Rockwall: Uncaged Publishing, 2013).

> *Like her other book, Thin Places, DeMuth portrays the enduring damage of childhood sexual abuse. But she doesn't leave you with the damage. She points to restoration and redemption. Although it can be difficult to read, I was left with a sense of hope.

Ken Graber, Ghosts in the Bedroom: A Guide for Partners of Incest Survivors (Deerfield Beach: Health Communications, Inc., 1991).

> *This is a book my husband read. It helped him to understand when I was being triggered by something and to understand that triggers could be anything and anywhere. He did feel it was too focused on intimacy and would have liked more focus on how to manage day-to-day.

Dawn Scott Jones, When a Woman You Love was Abused: A Husband's Guide to Helping Her Overcome Childhood Sexual Molestation (Grand Rapids: Kregel Publications, 2012).

> *This is written from the perspective of a survivor of childhood sexual abuse to a partner helping her through the journey. She discusses healing as a process rather than something that is quickly fixed.

Diane Mandt Langberg, Ph.D., On the Threshold of Hope: Opening the Door to Healing for Survivors of Sexual Abuse (Carol Stream: Tyndale House Publishers, Inc., 1999).

> *I found this book during the Wounded Hearts group. Diane Langberg has a heart for victims of sexual abuse. I found her writing to be a healing salve to my soul. The

words consistently point to a God who was grieved by what happened. Reading this book opened the door for me to wrestle the hard questions with God.

Cecil Murphey, When a Man You Love was Abused: A Woman's Guide to Helping Him Overcome Childhood Sexual Molestation (Grand Rapids: Kregel Publications, 2010).

*Like it's companion book, this book discusses the implications of childhood sexual abuse, but from the male perspective. It discusses the importance of a strong support system as well as the impact of childhood abuse on both partners in a marriage.

Philip Yancey, Where is God When It Hurts? (Grand Rapids: Zondervan, 1991).

*I turned to this book during a depressive period. Yancey highlights that our perception of pain and suffering is often short-sighted. He talks about suffering as a pathway to growth. When I learned to lean into my pain, I experienced growth in ways that I never thought possible. The fears of my childhood didn't vanish; however, they no longer controlled me.

For the Professional Helper

"Adverse Childhood Experiences," Substance Abuse and Mental Health Services Administration (SAMHSA), last modified May 1, 2017, https://www.samhsa.gov/capt/practicing-effective-prevention/prevention-behavioral-health/adverse-childhood-experiences.

Deborah A. Lee and Sophie James, The Compassionate Mind-Guide to Recovering from Trauma and PTSD (Oakland: New Harbinger Publications, Inc., 2011).

Bessel van der Kolk, The Body Keeps the Score: Brain, Mind, and Body in the Healing of Trauma (New York: Penguin Random House, LLC, 2014).

www.ingramcontent.com/pod-product-compliance
Lightning Source LLC
LaVergne TN
LVHW051518070426
835507LV00023B/3176